YOUR BRAIN ON FOOD

YOUR BRAIN

on

FOOD

HOW CHEMICALS CONTROL YOUR THOUGHTS AND FEELINGS

Gary L. Wenk, PhD
Departments of Psychology and Neuroscience and
Molecular Virology, Immunology and Medical Genetics
The Ohio State University
Columbus, OH

OXFORD
UNIVERSITY PRESS

2010

OXFORD
UNIVERSITY PRESS

Oxford University Press, Inc., publishes works that further
Oxford University's objective of excellence
in research, scholarship, and education.

Oxford   New York
Auckland   Cape Town   Dar es Salaam   Hong Kong   Karachi
Kuala Lumpur   Madrid   Melbourne   Mexico City
Nairobi   New Delhi   Shanghai   Taipei   Toronto

With offices in
Argentina   Austria   Brazil   Chile   Czech Republic   France   Greece
Guatemala   Hungary   Italy   Japan   Poland   Portugal   Singapore
South Korea   Switzerland   Thailand   Turkey   Ukraine   Vietnam

Published by Oxford University Press, Inc.
198 Madison Avenue, New York, New York 10016

www.oup.com

Oxford is a registered trademark of Oxford University Press.

Library of Congress Cataloging-in-Publication Data
Wenk, Gary Lee.
Your brain on food : how chemicals control your thoughts and feelings/
Gary L. Wenk.
p. ; cm.
ISBN 978-0-19-538854-1
1. Psychopharmacology. 2. Neuropsychology. 3. Neurochemistry. I. Title.
[DNLM: 1. Brain—physiology. 2. Emotions. 3. Neurotransmitter
Agents—physiology. WL 300 W475y 2010]
RM315.W46 2010
615'.78—dc22
2009047354

3 5 7 9 8 6 4 2
Printed in the United States of America
on acid-free paper

for Jane

CONTENTS

V arious writers over the past century have compared the human brain to an elegant machine. Imagine that this machine is full of wires and that the wires are different-colored. Some are blue, some are red, some are green, and so on, but they all convey information from one part of the machine to another. Now imagine that the blue wires are organized differently than the red wires, that the red wires are organized differently than the green wires, and so on. If you were to look inside your brain, you would discover that although its pathways are organized like the colored wires in your telephone or computer, it doesn't actually use wires at all but instead uses cells, or neurons, to process information: One neuron is connected to the next and to the next, and so on. Indeed, this elegant machine, your brain, is composed of approximately 100 billion neurons, and within a single structure, the cortex, these neurons make an estimated 0.15 quadrillion connections with each other. These billions of neurons are not uniquely colored, but they do release unique chemicals, called neurotransmitters, onto each other. What happens when molecules of a foreign substance—say, a drug or a morsel of food—interact with the neurons in this elegant machine? What happens to their neurotransmitters and, as a result, to you?

The major point that I want to make in this book is that anything you consume—the drugs you take, the foods you eat—can affect how your neurons behave and, subsequently, how you think and feel. In the course of illustrating this point, I examine what neuroscientists currently know about the actions of specific drugs and food in the brain and seek to advance your understanding of your own brain by demonstrating how its workings can be altered by what you "feed" it. Thus, I describe several neurotransmitter systems, including a little about their basic role in the brain, and explore how various substances—be they plant extracts, nuts, mushrooms, spices, chocolate, or medicinal and recreational drugs—can influence these neurotransmitters in terms of their production, their release from the neuron, and their ultimate inactivation and excretion from the body. I also discuss the brain's role in certain experiences—for example, hallucinations, religiosity, pain, and the aging process—and the extent to which these experiences are influenced by what we consume. In addition, I consider the role of evolution in determining the brain's responses to the food and drugs that we consume and place the use of some of these substances in cultural history.

The brain contains over 100 known, or suspected, neurotransmitter chemicals and probably as many that have not yet been discovered. I have chosen to focus on those neurotransmitter systems most commonly associated with the psychoactive effects of drugs and nutrients that, in many cases, are regularly consumed today. In general, I discuss mostly brain stimulants in the first half of the book and mostly depressants in the second half, although, as you will see, this dividing line is far from hard and fast, mainly because the brain does not always behave in such a dichotomous manner. Therefore, some stimulants appear later in the book; some depressants appear earlier; and some substances that influence a given neurotransmitter discussed in one chapter turn up again as they relate to neurotransmitters discussed in other chapters. However, there is a constant across these chapters: I've tried to organize much of the information about specific neurotransmitter systems according to the action of two types of substances—those that mimic these systems, thereby acting as agonists, and those that block them, thereby acting as antagonists. These and other fundamental concepts in pharmacology, as well as information about the basic neuroscience of the brain, are further explained in Chapter 1. In contrast, I have deliberately paid little or no attention to substances that have psychoactive effects on the brain but whose mechanism(s) of action have not yet been adequately defined in the scientific literature, such as lithium. Furthermore, I have made no attempt to detail the many, still poorly understood, additional roles played by the neurotransmitters that I do discuss.

In essence, this book is intended not as an exhaustive review of all that is known about the topic of drugs and the brain but as a brief—and, I hope, enjoyable—introduction to it. By the end of the book, you will know more than just how a select group of drugs or food works in your brain, you will be able to predict how substances that I did not discuss, and those that have not even been invented yet, might also affect your brain. Even better, you may look back on the chapters you've read and discover that they are much too simplistic for you now and that you want to learn more about greater complexities of brain function than this book covers. If reading this book motivates you to learn more about neuroscience and its associated topics, then I will have succeeded in my goal to advance your understanding of your brain. The suggested readings that I've listed at the end of the book offer an excellent next step in that advancement.

This book could not have been written without the encouragement and generosity of my mentors, colleagues, family, and friends—particularly David Olton, who patiently motivated my curiosity in the effects of drugs on the brain; James McGaugh, who inspired my interest in behavioral pharmacology; Giancarlo Pepeu, who has continued to nurture my interest in the role of drugs in the history of culture; Peabo Bryson, who challenged me to explore the role of neuroscience in religion; Paul Gold, for the many thought-provoking discussions on the Utah slopes; and Jacqueline Crawley, for her boundless enthusiasm and stimulating insights into the function of the brain. Their wisdom helped focus my fanciful ideas into rational theories. I will always be grateful to Catharine Carlin at Oxford University Press for her unflagging support and optimism at the beginning of this long journey. I also feel very privileged to have worked with Marion Osmun, my editor, who provided a nurturing combination of advice, encouragement, and bracing perspective. I am also grateful to the thousands of students who have taken my psychopharmacology classes and whose personal stories enliven these pages. Finally, for more than 30 years, I have been blessed to share my life with a woman of unrivaled intelligence and uncommon patience. Her profound personal wisdom has enriched my life in countless ways. This book is dedicated to Jane.

YOUR BRAIN ON FOOD

CHAPTER I

INTRODUCTION

Food, Drugs, and You

A long time ago, our ancestors discovered that ingesting some plants or the body parts of certain animals produced effects that were rather unpleasant or even lethal. Reference to these substances once appeared in a collection of prayers of comfort for the dying and referred to a type of spiritual medicine, at the time called a *pharmakon*, which was used principally to alleviate suffering near the end of life. Simply put, a pharmakon was a poison. Originally, the term *pharmakos* (φαρμακος) referred to a human scapegoat, who was sacrificed, sometimes literally by poisoning, as a remedy for the illness of another person, usually someone far more important in the local society. Later, around 600 BCE, the term came to refer to substances used to cure the sick. It is of course related to two terms now in use today: *pharmacology*, the scientific investigation into the mechanisms by which drugs affect the body, and *psychopharmacology*, the study of the effects of drugs upon the brain—effects that in turn are defined as "psychoactive."

This book explores not only several drugs but also a range of foods with these effects. In fact, the single unifying property of these substances is that they are all psychoactive in some way; they can affect your brain and therefore your behavior. By the end of the book, I hope that you will appreciate that the distinction between what is considered a drug (i.e., something that your brain wants or needs to function optimally) and food (i.e., something that your body wants or needs to function optimally) is becoming increasingly difficult to define. Indeed, the routine use of some substances, such as stimulants and depressants, is so universal that most of us do not even consider them to be drugs but, rather, actual food. Is coffee, tea, tobacco, alcohol, cocoa, or marijuana a nutrient or a drug? For many people, the distinction has become rather blurred. I suggest that anything you take into your body should be considered a drug, whether it's obviously nutritious or not. As you will see, even molecules that are clearly nutritious, such as essential amino acids like lysine and tryptophan (which can be purchased in any grocery store today), exhibit properties that many of us would attribute to a drug.

A SHARED EVOLUTIONARY HISTORY

The foods we eat and many of our most popular psychoactive drugs often come from plants. This fact has led scientists to recognize that the ingredients in these plants are very similar to the neurotransmitters our brains and bodies use to function normally. This is why the contents of our diets can interact with our neurons to influence brain function, and it highlights a very important principle: The food or drug that you consume will only act upon your brain if in some way that substance resembles an actual neurotransmitter or if it is able to interact with an essential biochemical process in your brain that influences the production, release, or inactivation of a neurotransmitter. The active ingredients in plants, or their extracts, that we consume are often only slightly modified amino acids that are very similar to those used by our brains.

How is it possible that plants and humans use such similar chemicals for normal, everyday functions? Plants produce chemicals that are capable of affecting our brain because they share an evolutionary history with us on this planet. Even primitive one-celled organisms produce many of the same chemicals that are in our brains. Therefore, whether you choose to eat a bunch of broccoli or a large pile of amoeba, the chemicals they contain may alter how your neurons function and, therefore, how you feel or think.

We have all experienced the consequences of our shared evolutionary history with the plants we eat. For example, unripe bananas contain the neurotransmitter serotonin. When you eat an unripe banana, its serotonin is free to act upon the serotonin neurons within your intestines. The consequence is likely to be increased activation of the muscles in the wall of your intestines, usually experienced as diarrhea.

Plants are not the only source of chemicals that can act upon your brain. The fact that you share an evolutionary history with insects and reptiles also underlies the ability of venoms, which often also contain serotonin, to produce unpleasant effects that you would feel if you were stung by a bee or bitten by a snake. Our shared history with plants and animals on earth leads to some interesting predictions. For example, consider the following science fiction scenario: A spaceman is walking on an Earth-like planet and is suddenly bitten by an unfriendly and grizzly looking creature. The space-man can see that he is injured and that a liquid substance was injected under his skin by the beast. Does he die? No, he does not die, because his species and that of the creature on this foreign planet do not share an evolutionary past or a common ancestor. Although their amino acids might have first evolved in space, as is now believed, since that distant time, their inde-pendent evolutionary paths have made it highly improbable that they use similar neurotransmitter molecules within their respective brains and bodies. Thus, every spaceman from Flash Gordon to Captain Kirk to Luke Skywalker should feel safe walking around any planet (except their own) with impunity from animal and plant toxins. For this same reason, the intoxi-cating drinks and powerful medicines that always seem to be popular on these foreign worlds in science fiction movies would also be completely without effect on the brains of our plucky spaceman.

DRUGS AND THE ORGAN OF THE MIND

Back on Earth, people in ancient cultures were certainly very aware of the unique properties of certain plants and of the consequences of consuming them on the body and brain; indeed, they often sought them out as remedies for a variety of physical illnesses. This ancient use of plant extracts as medicines was also likely the beginning of a long series of upheavals in our concept of how the brain functions and what its role is as the organ of the mind. For millennia, people believed that mental illness was caused by evil spirits or was a punishment delivered by an angry deity rather than as the result of a brain disease or dysfunction, as we now realize. Only comparatively recently, in the mid-20th century, have effective drugs been introduced for the treatment of mental illness. The realization that it might be possible to treat mental illness in the same way that one treated physical illness—that is, medically—was slow to gain general approval in part because of the wide-ranging, and for some quite frightening, implications about what this meant regarding the nature of the human mind. What if all mental activity is biochemical in nature? What if our cherished thoughts, such as of God, and our deepest emotions, such as love, are simply the result of biochemical reactions within one of the organs of our body? What does this say about the soul or romance? Will we one day have drugs to treat the broken soul or the broken heart similar to the drugs we use now to treat serious mental illness? It's probably not too farfetched to expect that yes, in the future, drugs will be invented to enhance our romantic urges (Viagra aside) and assist our communication with our deity of choice. Our grandchildren will likely have a whole host of drugs to enhance a broad range of mental functions.

In fact, we already do have a vast pharmacopeia, legal and otherwise, that affect the brain and no end of debate about their value and effectiveness. This leads me to several basic principles that apply to any substance you ingest that might affect your brain.

First, these substances should not be viewed as being either "good" or "bad." Drugs and nutrients in your diet are simply chemicals—no more, no less. They have actions within your brain that you either desire or would like to avoid. Second, every drug has multiple effects. Because your brain and body are so complex and because the chemicals you ingest are free to act in many different areas of your brain and body at the same time, they will often have many different effects—both direct and indirect—on your brain function and behavior. Third, the effect of a drug or nutrient on your brain always depends on the amount consumed. Varying the dose of any particular drug changes the magnitude and the character of its effects. This principle is called the dose–response effect—that is, in general, greater doses lead to greater effects on your brain, although sometimes greater doses produce completely opposite effects than low doses. Finally, the effects of a drug on your brain are greatly influenced by your genes, the nature of the drug-taking

experience, and the expectations that you have about the consequences of the experience. For example, if you respond strongly
to one drug, you're likely to respond strongly to many drugs,
and this trait is likely shared by at least one of your parents.

Sometimes the contribution of your genes to your drug
experience can be dangerous. One young man in my class wanted
to pledge to a popular fraternity, but he was rather awkward
socially and had trouble making friends. He began attending
fraternity parties, and against the warnings of his parents, he
started drinking alcohol and smoking marijuana cigarettes. He
reported that he became paralyzed after he drank alcohol. It was
an odd paralysis that would disappear after a few hours. In the
meantime, other students at the party would place his limbs in
odd positions, where they remained until the paralysis passed.
I asked a physician friend about his condition and learned that
the student had probably inherited a disorder of alcohol metabolism. His body converted alcohol into a derivative that was
quite toxic to his muscles and so irritating to them that they
produced a tonic grip on his body. If he had continued drinking alcohol, then the cellular debris from his degenerating
muscles would slowly have collected inside his kidneys, causing
them to fail as well. The interaction of his genes and alcohol
was going to have devastating effects on his health if he did not
quickly change his behavior. There are at least two lessons we
can take from this student's nearly disastrous experience. First,
get to know your genetic history—you might have some hidden
surprises waiting to be uncovered. Second, sometimes, a little

basic knowledge about how the things we consume can affect our bodies can actually save our lives.

REALLY BASIC NEUROSCIENCE AND PHARMACOLOGY

Just how food and drugs affect the brain is the focus of this book, and in subsequent chapters we examine the details underlying the specific mechanisms involved in this process. But to ground that discussion, we need first to consider some very basic anatomy and chemistry involving the brain and to generally define the key mechanisms involved in brain–drug interactions.

Why are our brains located in our heads? Wouldn't they be safer if they were deep in our chest, similar to the location of our hearts? Brains, regardless of how small or simple, have evolved at the best possible location to perform their principal function: survival of the individual and the species. With very few exceptions, brains are always located at the front end of an animal's feeding "tube" or mechanism, which in humans and many other organisms is the tubular system (the alimentary canal) that extends from the mouth to the anus. Your brain makes it possible for you to find food by sight, sound, and smell and then to organize your behavior so that the front end of your feeding tube can get close enough to taste the food and check it for beneficial or potentially harmful contents before you ingest it. Once the food is in your feeding tube, it is absorbed and becomes available to the cells of your body. Your entire feeding tube and associated organs, also known as the gastrointestinal system, use nearly 70% of the energy you consume just to make the remaining 30% available to the rest of your body. Your brain uses about 14% of the available consumed energy, and your other organs that allow you to reproduce and move around your environment (including your muscles and bones) utilize about 15%. As you can see, very little energy is left over for other tasks in the body. These percentages give you some idea of the priorities—sex and mobility—that billions of years of evolution have set for your body to achieve.

Big brains use a lot of energy, and therefore their evolution depended first on building large feeding tubes. Later, the forces of evolution changed strategies and depended on the development of a more efficient and somewhat shorter feeding tube. Thus, today we have a big brain and a gastrointestinal system that is fairly efficient at extracting energy for itself and its principal customer: the brain. If we reproduced asexually, our brain's job would mostly be done after orchestrating that activity. But we're not asexual creatures, and so our brain must use most of its available energy to organize our behavior so that we can socialize with others in our species and find a mate with whom to produce children. That's our inherent biological imperative anyway, whether or not everyone in our species responds to it.

You know one manifestation of this imperative as dating, and it requires a very, very large and complex brain to pull off successfully. Meanwhile, your brain has evolved some interesting neurotransmitter chemicals that allow you to enjoy dating—two, in particular, are dopamine and an opium-like chemical.

Both play a critical role in rewarding your brain—and therefore you—for consuming high-calorie food, such as the quintessential dating meal of cheeseburgers and fries at the local diner, and for having sex, often the quintessential dating result. Eating and having sex are obviously excellent ideas if your purpose is to maintain and propagate your species. But these two neurotransmitters, as you'll learn in later chapters, play a larger role in allowing you to experience happiness or euphoria through various behaviors, whether you're eating donuts, having sex, or shooting heroin.

Okay, let's return to the anatomy lesson. At this point, you need only appreciate that your brain is composed of neurons and some supporting cells, called *glia*. If you were to extract a very small cube of brain tissue (*see* Fig. 1–1), you would find it densely packed with cells, blood vessels, and very little else. The neurons are organized into columns of cells and small gatherings, called *nuclei* or *ganglia*, which tend to be involved in related functions. For example, some ganglia control movement, some control body temperature, and some control your mood.

Overall, your brain is organized so that the back half receives incoming sensory information and then processes and organizes it into your own very personal experience of the here and now. The front half of your brain is responsible for planning and movement, usually in response to some important incoming sensory stimulus, such as someone's voice telling you that it's time for dinner. You hear the voice, smell the aroma of food cooking, feel a craving for food as your blood sugar levels fall,

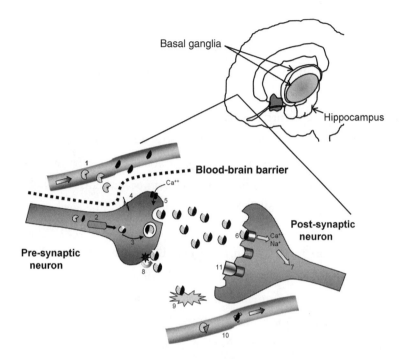

Figure 1–1. Top: The anatomy of a few brain regions that will be discussed later. Bottom: How individual neurons communicate with each other. See text for details.

sense that it's late in the day and the sun is setting, and so on; thus, it must be dinnertime. This information is funneled into the front of your brain, which then makes a decision to move the front end of your feeding tube toward the smell and the voice to obtain a reward—the food and survival for another day!

To facilitate the process between your sensing the external world and deciding how to interact with it and to elicit useful behaviors that will improve your chances of survival, propagate your species, and make you happy, the neurons in your brain must communicate with each other; they do this mostly by releasing neurotransmitters onto each other, including the two neurotransmitters just mentioned as well as others that will be introduced shortly. Most of them can be found in just about every brain structure. Moreover, their function depends entirely on the function of the structures in which they are located.

Let's take a look at a few examples. First, find the basal ganglia in Figure 1–1. The nuclei that compose the basal ganglia are responsible for allowing normal movement. The level of the neurotransmitter dopamine in these nuclei is much higher than in most surrounding brain regions. Therefore, scientists have concluded that dopamine within the basal ganglia is involved in the control of movement. Furthermore, if we expose your brain to a drug that impairs the function of dopamine or the neurons that produce and release it, then your ability to move will be impaired. But it would be incorrect to assume that dopamine is always involved with movement— it is not. You can also find dopamine in the retina of your eye and in your hypothalamus, structures that have nothing to do movement. Similarly, the neurotransmitter norepinephrine can be found in the hippocampus, a structure critical for forming new memories. Thus, norepinephrine influences the formation of memories. However, norepinephrine plays a role in other brain regions that have nothing to do with making memories. The take away point is that there is no such thing as a specifically unique "dopamine function" or an exclusively distinct "norepinephrine function." The brain region that the neurotransmitter is found within defines its function, not the neurotransmitter itself. In fact, neurotransmitters exhibit a complex array of actions in different brain regions, and so you can rarely make a single universal statement about their role in brain function.

Neurotransmitters are produced in our brains from the contents of our diets by means of a many-step process. First, nutrients (labeled 1 in Fig. 1–1), such as amino acids, sugar, fats, and peptides (strings of amino acids bound together), are extracted and absorbed from the food we eat and are transported out of the arterial blood supply to the brain—that is, they are actively carried through the blood–brain barrier and transported into the neurons. Enzymes (2) convert these nutrients into different neurotransmitters. The neurotransmitter molecules are actively transported into what are called synaptic vesicles (3), or very tiny spheres with hollow centers into which about 10,000 molecules of a typical neurotransmitter can be stored for later release from a neuron.

The arrival of an electrical signal (4) then initiates a series of further steps. This electrical signal is called an action potential. It is a very small electrical disturbance that moves very quickly along the axon away from the cell body. The axon is a long, straight extension of the neuron that carries the action potential and allows one neuron to communicate with other neurons. Axons are rather like electrical wires that connect the different parts of the brain. The arrival of the action potential at the end of the axon induces the entry of calcium ions, which initiate the next step in the communication of one neuron with the next: a synaptic vessel merges into its cell wall (imagine two soap bubbles coming together) and releases (5) the neurotransmitter into a very small space between neurons, called a synaptic cleft. The junction at which two neurons communicate via the release of a neurotransmitter molecule is called a synapse. The neurotransmitter molecule briefly interacts or binds with a protein, called a receptor (6), on the surface of the neuron on the other side of the synapse. One consequence of this binding action is that some ions, such as calcium (Ca^{++}) or sodium (Na^+), move into the downstream neuron to induce secondary biochemical processes (7), which may have long-term consequences on the neuron's behavior.

Meanwhile, after interacting with the receptor, the actions of the neurotransmitter must be terminated by means of its reabsorption (8) back into the neuron that originally released it. This is called reuptake. A secondary method of neurotransmitter inactivation is by enzymatic conversion (9) into a chemical that can no longer interact with your brain. Once the neurotransmitter is enzymatically inactivated, it is removed from the brain into the bloodstream (10). Such byproducts of the ordinary hustle and bustle of the brain can be easily monitored in many of our body fluids, and this information can be used to determine whether our brains are functioning normally.

Drugs and the contents of our diet can interact with any of these various processes and impair, or even sometimes enhance, the production of neurotransmitters, as well as impair their storage into synaptic vesicles, alter their release from neurons, modify their interaction with receptor proteins (identified as 11 in Fig. 1–1), slow their reuptake, and possibly even stop their enzymatic inactivation. Because your brain is the organ of the mind, drugs and foods that do any of these things can have a profound influence on how you think, act, and feel. The remainder of this book focuses on these actions and on what they tell you about your own brain.

How do drugs and chemicals in our diet actually affect our brains? Most drugs influence the transmission of chemical signals between neurons. The part of your brain or body where a drug acts to produce its effect is called the drug's "site of action." The behavioral effects of a drug can provide clues to its site of action within your brain. For example, drugs that affect your sleep or your level of arousal usually alter activity of neurons within a region of your brain that is called the brainstem-activating system. Another clue to a drug's site of action is provided by the unequal distribution of neurotransmitters in the brain. For example, as mentioned earlier, dopamine is highly concentrated in the basal ganglia, a part of the brain that controls movement. Therefore, drugs that affect the dopamine system often impair movement.

Why do some drugs and chemicals in our diets affect our brains and how we feel while others have no effect on us? Many drugs that might potentially influence brain function are never able to enter the brain because of the presence of a series of barriers; the most important of these is the blood–brain barrier. This barrier allows the easy entry of drugs that are lipid (fat)-soluble and restricts the entry of drugs that are water-soluble. Because the brain is composed of so many lipids, the tendency of a drug to dissolve into lipid and water phases of the brain tells us much about how a drug achieves its effects. Very lipid-soluble drugs enter the brain rapidly; they also tend to exit rather rapidly, which reduces the duration of their action. Some familiar examples of lipid-soluble drugs are the vitamins A, D, E and K. Nicotine and caffeine are also quite lipid-soluble and enter the brain easily; if they did not, then it is highly unlikely that anyone would be abusing them. Take a moment to appreciate how this fact has been an incredible boon to the evolutionary success of tobacco and coffee plants: Their discovery by our species led to their widespread cultivation and protection as two of the most important plants on earth.

Once a drug has entered the brain, what happens next? Most of the time, the site of action is a receptor protein, which floats on the surface of a neuron. Drugs that bind to receptors and produce a reaction by the neuron are typically called agonists; drugs that bind to receptors and effectively block the action of a neurotransmitter or agonist are called antagonists. Put another way, agonists usually stimulate a response from the neuron, and antagonists usually prevent or reduce the response of neurons. These two terms are used frequently throughout the book.

Some drugs that you might consume are never completely metabolized or inactivated after they have entered your body and are therefore available to re-enter your brain and continue to affect brain function. In contrast, some chemicals that you

ingest are actually metabolized by your body into quite powerful psychoactive drugs. For example, a small percentage of the
codeine in cough syrup is converted into morphine, a far more
powerful painkiller; psilocybin, from the hallucinogenic mushroom of the same name, is converted into the equally hallucinogenic psilocin; heroin is inactive in your brain and must be
converted into morphine before it can produce its euphoric
effects. Usually, however, a drug is converted by enzymes to
make it inactive in your brain and body and is subsequently
excreted in the urine, feces, sweat, breast milk, or expired air
from the lungs.

Sometimes the effects of a drug are present for so long that
the brain slowly adjusts to their presence. Over time, the brain
acts as though the drug has become a necessary component of
normal brain function. You experience your brain's adjustment
to the eventual absence of this substance as craving.

What does craving feel like? Consider, for example, the very
powerful drug sugar. Your brain needs sugar (usually in the form
of glucose) to function normally. The many billions of neurons
in your brain require a constant supply of glucose to maintain
their ability to produce energy and communicate with other
neurons. These neurons can only tolerate a deprivation of glucose for a few minutes before they begin to die. Therefore, as
blood levels of sugar decrease with the passage of time since
your last meal, you begin to experience a craving for food, prefer-
ably something sweet. The presence of sugar in your brain is
considered normal, and its absence leads to the feeling of craving

and the initiation of hunting or foraging behaviors, such as seeking out a vending machine for a Hershey Bar. If you wish to experience the truly overwhelming and powerful nature of drug craving, just stop eating for a full day.

A second, and far less familiar, example of craving would be the response of the brain to long-term exposure to the drug amphetamine. This drug increases the release of the neurotransmitters dopamine, norepinephrine, and serotonin from neurons. The constant presence of these neurotransmitters within the synapse modifies the number and behavior of neuronal protein receptors. Over time and with daily exposure to amphetamine, the behavior of various neurons changes in profound ways. These compensatory changes partly explain why people who use amphetamine often require greater and greater amounts of the drug to experience a consistent feeling of euphoria. After a few hours, when amphetamine levels in the brain decrease, the individual experiences a lack of euphoria, or dysphoria, which will be experienced as depression and a craving for the return of amphetamine back into the brain. The brain, in short, craves chemicals that it "thinks" it needs to function normally. At this point, the continued craving is called an addiction.

The constant consumption of caffeine, nicotine, or almost any chemical can produce similar types of compensatory changes within your brain and lead to craving with their absence from the brain. This kind of response is exactly what your brain evolved to do for you: its purpose is to be flexible and learn how to survive, to be plastic or adaptive to a changing environment and to the variety of chemicals that enter your feeding tube. When this situation of "normalcy" is lost because of the absence of something that your brain has become accustomed to having regularly available (e.g., sugar, amphetamine, or anything else that you're accustomed to consuming), your brain reacts by creating in you the urge to replenish its supply. You experience this feeling as craving, regardless of the legality, safety, or cost of the substance being craved.

Craving is also associated with another interesting expression of brain function. The removal of a drug from the brain is frequently accompanied by biological and behavioral changes that are opposite to those produced by the drug: this is rebound. I like to say that the brain always "pushes back." For example, the rebound from the euphoria induced by the stimulants cocaine and amphetamine is the depression that follows once the drugs have left the brain. This interesting brain response is apparently only unidirectional. What I mean by this is that we often observe depression following stimulant-induced euphoria, but we never see euphoria as part of the rebound experience following use of depressants such as alcohol and barbiturates. No one ever experiences happiness as part of a hangover from a night of binge drinking!

Many biological factors such as age and weight play a crucial role in the way that drugs affect the brain and influence behavior. So, too, does the unique neural circuitry that you inherited from your parents and that sometimes influences whether a drug will be exciting or depressing to you. This concept was probably best described as the "Law of Initial Value" by Joseph Wilder in 1958 in the *American Journal of Psychotherapy*. The law states that each person has an initial level of excitation that is determined by his or her genetics, physiology, sickness or health status, drug history, and environmental factors; the degree of response to a psychoactive drug depends on how all of these factors affect one's current level of excitation or melancholy. For example, patients suffering from pain, anxiety, or tension experience euphoria when they are given small doses of morphine. In contrast, a similar dose of morphine given to a happy, pain-free individual often precipitates mild anxiety and fear. If you have a fever, aspirin lowers your body temperature, but aspirin cannot cool your body on a hot day—you must first have the fever for it to work. Coffee produces elation and improves your ability to pay attention if you have been awake for a long period of time or had poor sleep the night before; in contrast, the same dose of coffee is likely to produce much less arousal if you are well-rested. Catatonic patients may respond with a burst of animation and spontaneity to an intravenous injection of barbiturates, whereas most people would simply fall asleep. Sedative drugs create more anxiety in outgoing, athletic people than they do in introverted intellectual types.

The Law of Initial Value is a fascinating, and largely underappreciated, concept worthy of additional discussions that are beyond the scope of this book. Indeed, the various basics of neuroscience and pharmacology just summarized barely scratch the surface of all that has been learned over the years about the brain and its response to drugs. The chapters that follow build on these basics a bit further to examine the intersection of brain anatomy, brain chemistry, evolution, and culture. Along the way, we examine some of the major neurotransmitter systems in detail. Of these, I begin with the neurotransmitter that pharmacologist Otto Loewi discovered a couple days after Easter Sunday in 1920 while working at University College, London. His equipment was simple but his insights demonstrated true genius. Loewi shared the Nobel Prize for Physiology or Medicine in 1936 with Henry Dale, also a pharmacologist, for their work on chemical neurotransmission, and so it is fitting that I begin with the focus of this work, acetylcholine.

CHAPTER 2

MEMORIES, MAGIC, & A MAJOR ADDICTION

W hat causes memory loss in patients with Alzheimer's disease? Why did witches once believe that they could fly? Why is it so hard to stop smoking? The answers to these questions can be found by understanding the function of acetylcholine, a neurotransmitter chemical that exists almost everywhere in nature. It has been found in both uni- and multi-cellular organisms, including in a strain of *Pseudomonas fluorescens* isolated from the juice of fermenting cucumbers, as well as in the blue-green algae, *Oscillatoria agardhii*, where it may be involved with photosynthesis. Acetylcholine stimulates silk production in spiders and limb regeneration in salamanders. In humans, acetylcholine enables movement by stimulating the muscles to contract, and it plays an important role in the action of the parasympathetic and sympathetic nervous systems, which are part of the autonomic nervous system (ANS). The ANS maintains homeostasis, or a balance of forces or equilibrium, for your entire body. Among other functions, it controls the rate at which your heart beats, how fast you breathe, how much saliva your mouth is making, the rate of movement of material in your gut, your ability to initiate urination, how much you are perspiring, the size of your pupils, and the degree of visible sexual excitation you might experience. Within the human brain are numerous acetylcholine pathways that influence the function of the cortex, hippocampus, and many other regions (see Fig. 2–1). Within these various regions, the actions of acetylcholine allow you to learn and remember, to regulate your attention and mood, and to control how well you can move. Thus, anything that affects the function of acetylcholine neurons has the potential to affect all of these brain and body functions. That "anything" could be a certain drug or a disease.

A CASE IN POINT: ALZHEIMER'S DISEASE

Sometimes we can learn much about the role of a particular neurotransmitter system by investigating what happens when it is injured or diseased. In the brains of people with Alzheimer's disease, for example, acetylcholine neurons that project into the hippocampus and cortex very slowly die. The effects of this neuronal death have been the subject of research in my laboratory for more than 25 years. The loss of normal acetylcholine function in the cortex may be why patients with Alzheimer's

Corpus collosum

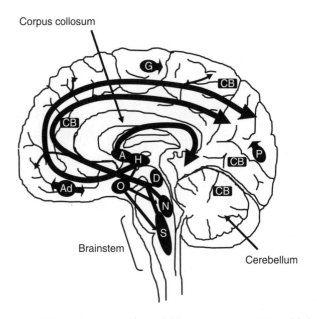

Brainstem

Cerebellum

Figure 2–1. Schematic anatomy of neurotransmitter systems. *A.* Acetylcholine neurons mostly originate within the basal forebrain region and project to the cortex, hippocampus, amygdala, and olfactory bulbs. *Ad.* Adenosine can be released by virtually every cell in the brain. *CB.* Cannabinoid neurons are scattered throughout the brain and cerebellum. *D.* Dopamine neurons originate within the midbrain project into the basal ganglia and frontal lobes. *G.* GABA neurons are found throughout the brain as small inter-neurons and also project from one brain region to another. *H.* Histamine neurons mostly lie near the bottom of the brain and project diffusely into most brain regions. *N.* Norepinephrine neurons originate within the locus coeruleus in the floor of the 4th ventricle, under the cerebellum, and project virtually everywhere in the brain. *O.* Orexin neurons that project onto acetylcholine, dopamine, histamine, serotonin, and norepinephrine neurons to promote wakefulness. *P.* Peptide-containing neurons tend to be diffusely scattered although there are notable exceptions. *S.* Serotonin neurons originate with a scattered group of nuclei that lie along the midline of the brainstem and project downward into the spinal cord and upward into all regions of the brain. Glutamate neurons are found everywhere in the brain; they are not represented in the figure.

disease have difficulty paying attention to their environment. The loss of acetylcholine projections to the amygdala, part of the brain's limbic system, may underlie the emotional instability, such as irritability and paranoia, that is sometimes observed in these patients. And the loss of acetylcholine projections into the hippocampus may underlie the profoundly debilitating memory loss that is the major hallmark of this disease.

Let me illustrate the effect of at least one of these losses by first describing the role of acetylcholine in the cortex of a normal brain (yours). Imagine that, using an electroencephalogram or EEG, I have attached some electrodes to the front half of your head to record the electrical activity occurring inside your brain. Next, I calmly inform you that as soon as I ring a bell (at the point in time shown by the number 1 in Fig. 2–2) a

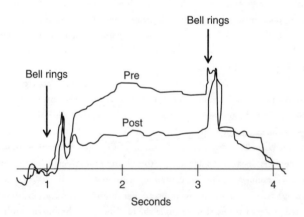

Figure 2–2. Electroencephalogram recorded over the frontal lobes showing the presence of an "anticipation wave" with an intact acetylcholine system (labeled *pre*) and without a functioning acetylcholine system (labeled *post*). The sharp vertical spikes are associated with a bell ringing at the beginning and end of the recording.

masked gunman will enter the room and start shooting. [You must also believe that I'm telling the truth for this to work.] Okay, now I ring the bell. Take a look at the EEG recording labeled "**pre**" in the figure. It shows that an electrical wave quickly appears within the frontal lobes of your brain that began as soon as I rang the bell. The bell ringing causes those sharp spikes prior to the formation of the wave. This electrical pattern, also known as an EEG wave, will continue to live in your brain until one of two things happens: either someone runs into the room with a gun (at the point in time shown by the number 3) or the bell rings again and you decide nothing is going to happen after all. At that point, the EEG wave will disappear. This **pre** wave indicates that you were paying close attention to what you thought was about to happen. It is an expression of your brain experiencing anticipation.

Experiments in my laboratory and in others have demonstrated that the appearance of this wave of electrical activity requires the normal function of acetylcholine within your frontal cortex. If the acetylcholine neurons that project into your frontal cortex are destroyed, then this wave cannot fully form and you will have great difficulty paying attention to important things, such as the impending appearance of a masked gunman. An example of such a wave is labeled "**post**" in the figure. In this case, the absence of acetylcholine does not allow the wave to fully develop. This research has demonstrated that acetylcholine's job is to instruct the neurons in your frontal cortex to pay attention to important information and be vigilant to impending danger. If acetylcholine function is impaired, this ability is lost. These results provide valuable insight into why patients with Alzheimer's disease have trouble paying attention to things that might be important, or even harmful, to them. Indeed, during the later stages of their disease, when most of these acetylcholine neurons have disappeared, patients have difficulty paying attention to anything at all.

ACETYLCHOLINE PRODUCTION AND RELEASE

Sometimes, the severity of the cognitive symptoms in Alzheimer's disease can be reduced, at least to some degree, by drugs and dietary nutrients that enhance the function of acetylcholine neurons in the brain. To understand how this is possible, we need to look at how acetylcholine is produced in the brain in the first place.

Neurons synthesize acetylcholine from *choline*, which is obtained from the diet, and from *acetyl* groups that originate in mitochondria from the metabolism of sugar. Here is yet another example of the importance of sugar for your brain's normal function. The synthesis of acetylcholine occurs within the cytoplasm of your neurons, and the product is stored in synaptic vesicles, those small round packets that neurons release to communicate with each other. Neurons pay a lot of attention to the shelf life of their neurotransmitters; they prefer to release the most recently produced neurotransmitter molecules first. As you can see, neurons do not behave like your local grocer: they do not rotate their stock. This means that the freshest products (the most recently produced acetylcholine molecules) are released first, thus guaranteeing that the communication between neurons is successful.

Many health food stores in malls across America sell choline powder to gullible customers, claiming that consuming more choline will somehow allow their brains to make more acetylcholine. Given the vital role of acetylcholine in learning and memory, this is an appealing claim. Regrettably, it has no basis in fact. For adults, the brain responds only to deficits, not surpluses, in the diet. It has a ready source of choline in the diet or stored in the liver and, in fact, never develops a deficit in choline, even in patients with Alzheimer's disease. Thus, consuming extra choline does not induce your brain to make more acetylcholine. Instead, it only results in a gaseous byproduct that you exhale and that smells like rotting fish. Rather than enhancing your cognitive abilities, choline supplements merely generate a terrible case of bad breath.

Once released, the action of acetylcholine within the synapse is terminated or inactivated by an enzyme called acetylcholinesterase at the rate of approximately 25,000 molecules per second. Thus, even the partial inhibition of this enzyme's activity has a profound effect on synaptic levels of acetylcholine. Many different drugs are capable of inhibiting this enzyme, including some nerve gases that cause synaptic levels of acetylcholine to rise too high and that are therefore highly poisonous as well as some drugs that cause the level to rise just enough to be clinically beneficial. Physostigmine, for example, is currently being given to patients with Alzheimer's disease to improve their ability to pay attention or remember the day's events, although sadly, its benefits tend to be very limited and they do not alter the ultimate course of the disease. Nonetheless, what the contrasting effects of these drugs have taught neuroscientists is that a little extra acetylcholine in the synaptic cleft between neurons seems to improve our thinking abilities, whereas too much acetylcholine can be lethal.

It's worth considering what would happen if a neuron could not release acetylcholine at all. The botulinum toxin from the *Clostridium botulinum* bacteria that sometimes forms in the foods we eat can inhibit the release of acetylcholine from nerve terminals. Fortunately for your brain, this toxin cannot cross the blood–brain barrier. But unfortunately, there's more to you than just your brain. Botulinum toxin can significantly impair the ability of your vagus nerve to control your breathing. Your vagus nerve is responsible for causing the contraction of your diaphragm muscle to pull air into your lungs (*see* Fig. 2–3). However, if your brain cannot communicate with your diaphragm via the release of acetylcholine from the vagus nerve, then you will stop breathing and die. The botulinum toxin is exceptionally potent; one gram is sufficient to kill approximately 350,000 people!

Once released into the synapse, the neurotransmitter acetylcholine can act on two quite different protein receptors that have been designated, as have most receptors, according to the compounds that were originally used to study them—in this

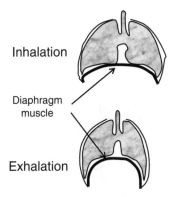

Figure 2–3. The release of acetylcholine onto the diaphragm muscle causes it to contract and pull air into the lungs (inspiration). The relaxation of this muscle allows air to leave the lungs (expiration).

case, muscarine and nicotine. Most of the acetylcholine (or "cholinergic") receptors in the brain are the muscarinic subtype, whereas less than 10% are nicotinic. Both types of receptors have been found in peanut worms (whose fossils date back a half-billion years), spoon worms, leeches, and earthworms. There is no evidence that these two receptors are related or share a common evolutionary history: They differ in size, structure, and mechanism of action; yet they both respond to acetylcholine.

Moreover, their response to different drugs tells us something important about the role that these two different acetylcholine receptors play in the brain and the body. Some drugs block, or antagonize, these receptors, whereas other drugs enhance, or stimulate (i.e., act as agonists of), them. Let's now look at several types of drugs to see what their actions reveal about the function of these receptors.

ANTAGONIZING ACETYLCHOLINE

Curare, found in a resinous extract of the plants *Chondrodendron tomentosum* and *Strychnos toxifera* from the Orinoco and Amazon basins in South America, is an antagonist at nicotinic acetylcholine receptors. Curare does not cross the blood–brain barrier, and therefore its actions are expressed only outside of the brain at the neuromuscular junction where neurons control muscles. Curare is extremely lethal for one simple reason—it blocks the nicotinic receptors located on the diaphragm; therefore, death from curare results from asphyxiation. Imagine you've been shot by a curare-tipped arrow: you'd be awake, fully aware of having been shot, yet completely unable to move, speak, or, ultimately, breathe.

The naturally occurring drugs atropine and scopolamine have a different sort of antagonistic effect: They block the muscarinic subtype of acetylcholine receptors. As a result, they impair our ability to form new memories and produce considerable mental confusion and drowsiness. At high doses, atropine and scopolamine can be lethal.

Several plants contain atropine and scopolamine, including henbane (*Hyoscyamus niger*), jimson weed (*Datura stramonium*), and mandrake (*Mandragora officinarum*). The "bane" part of henbane refers to an archaic Old English word for death; according to legend, local farmers noticed that their hens and roosters did not live long after eating this plant. Another plant, the "deadly nightshade" or *Atropa belladonna*, was given its name by the botanist Carl von Linné in the 18th century to signify its deadly nature. He derived the genus name from one of the Greek fates, Atropos, who cut the thread of life at the appointed time—she was death.

Poets and writers have long been aware of the lethal effects of these plants and have often incorporated them into their stories. For example, consider Shakespeare's tragedy *Hamlet*: King Hamlet of Denmark dies suddenly, ostensibly from snake-bite, and a few weeks later, his brother Claudius marries the king's widow, Queen Gertrude. The ghost of the king appears before his son, Prince Hamlet, and reveals that Claudius killed him by pouring into his ear the contents of an ampoule of henbane. In Act I, Scene 5, we find the ghost speaking to Hamlet:

> *"Sleeping within mine orchard, My custom always in the afternoon, Upon my secure hour thy uncle stole, With juice of cursed hebona [henbane] in a vial, And in the porches of mine ears did pour The leperous distilment; whose effect Holds such as enmity with blood of man."*

Enmity indeed!

How did scopolamine and atropine, both components of henbane, kill King Hamlet? To answer this, let's return to the autonomic nervous system. Recall the functions of the ANS that I mentioned previously. For example, it controls heart and breathing rate, intestinal motility, pupil dilation, salivation, and perspiration The two major components of the ANS, the parasympathetic and sympathetic nervous systems (see Fig. 2–4), essentially function in competition with each other to maintain

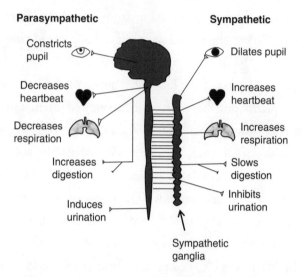

Figure. 2–4. The two major components of the ANS. The parasympathetic neurons release acetylcholine; the sympathetic neurons release norepinephrine. These two systems provide a balance of control of the function of the organs and structures shown.

a balance so that your heart does not beat too fast or too slow, you do not breathe too quickly or slowly, the contents of your gut do not move too fast or too slow, and so forth. When the parasympathetic nervous system is in control, it slows your heart rate, slows your breathing, constricts the pupils of your eyes, increases the production of saliva in your mouth, and so forth. When the sympathetic nervous system is in control, it increases your heart rate, increases your respiration rate, dilates the pupils of your eyes, reduces salivation (leaving you with a dry metallic taste in your mouth), and so forth. This careful dance between these two competing neural systems is choreographed by your brain, but you are usually not aware of it. However, when something disturbs this balance, such as scopolamine, you become very aware that something is wrong.

Recall that scopolamine, an ingredient in henbane, blocks muscarinic acetylcholine receptors. This blockade essentially removes the influence of the parasympathetic nervous system on the body. In the absence of this influence, the balance of forces is upset and the sympathetic nervous system gains the upper hand; thus, your heart rate increases, your pupils dilate, salivation stops, your ability to urinate is impaired, and you become constipated; overall, things get very uncomfortable. But none of this is directly lethal (unless the constipation makes one commit suicide). If you do die from an overdose of henbane, it is believed to result from either a complex series of events in your brain that lead to the loss of control of your diaphragm, causing death from asphyxiation, or from cardiac arrest. This is why the deadly nightshade is so deadly and how Shakespeare chose to kill King Hamlet with henbane.

An even earlier literary reference to the toxic effects of extracts from these types of plants appeared in Homer's *Odyssey*. Odysseus, the legendary king of Ithaca and hero of the poem, was advised to defend himself against the sorceress Circe's poison by eating a *"moly,"* which historians think refers to an extract of *Galanthus nivalis* or Snowdrop, a plant similar to henbane. Among the first bulbs to bloom in spring, the Snowdrop contains galanthamine, which can inhibit the enzyme acetylcholinesterase, much like physostigmine. By inhibiting acetylcholinesterase, the moly would increase the amount of acetylcholine in the synapse. The additional acetylcholine would be able to compete successfully with the poison for the acetylcholine receptor and prevent death. During Homer's time, a *moly* might have been a common antidote against poisonous plants containing scopolamine-like drugs. Ironically, extracts from scopolamine-containing plants, like the *Datura,* may also have been used as antidotes to poisoning from eating the Snowdrop plant, proving correct once again the words of the Roman poet Lucretius, "One man's poison is another man's antidote."

Simply stated, it is just as dangerous to have too much acetylcholine in the synapse as it is to have too little. During World War II, German chemical companies produced nerve gases that were based on the action of the Snowdrop plant and thus were very potent inhibitors of the acetylcholinesterase enzyme. During battle, these gases were designed to be sprayed into the air and then inhaled by soldiers who would quickly become unable to walk or breathe and would ultimately die. Just as the Greeks seem to have discovered two millennia earlier, the soldiers could defend against this poison by injecting themselves with extracts from the *Datura* plant. But timing was everything: The soldiers could safely inject the extracts only if they suspected imminent exposure to a nerve gas. Otherwise the use of this antidote could backfire if no gas attack occurred. Imagine an entire brigade of soldiers infused with scopolamine: they'd be fully amnesic, unable to urinate, and mentally confused—not exactly the characteristics of an effective combat unit. Indeed, this is exactly what may have led to the defeat of Marc Antony's army by the Parthians in 36 BCE.

Many of the most effective insecticides available today are based on the same biochemical mechanism of the nerve gases—that is, the potent inhibition of the enzyme acetylcholinesterase. These chemicals are effective as insecticides because insects, who share our evolutionary history on this planet, are also vulnerable to having too much acetylcholine in their synapses.

VOODOO DOLLS, HALLUCINATIONS, AND BEAUTY

This seems as good a place as any to touch on the truly weird to highlight other details relating to antagonists of muscarinic acetylcholine receptors. Voodoo death and the creation of zombies, although not completely well understood as phenomena, are a great illustration of the workings of the ANS. Voodoo itself is a complex religion derived from West African polytheism and is practiced primarily in Haiti. I wish to focus on that famous effigy of vengeance that most people associate with the term: the voodoo doll, into which one person sticks spikes or pins as part of a curse on another person. For people who truly believe in the power of the voodoo doll, the fear that this curse generates in the victim is usually quite powerful. The physiological expressions of this fear result from the extreme activation of the sympathetic nervous system. The unfortunate victim begins to experience uncomfortable heart palpitations, sweating, dry mouth, and heavy breathing that leads to a loss of carbon dioxide, and, as a consequence, lightheadedness. This physical condition plays into the person's fear and expectations of what should be happening as a result of this curse; these thoughts produce more fear and more sympathetic ANS activation.

Unless the person suffers a heart attack resulting from some sort of underlying, undiagnosed heart condition, this extremely fearful experience is not usually lethal. Instead, the excessive activation of the sympathetic nervous system triggers a compensatory reflex that is called the baroreceptor reflex, which results in an abrupt drop in heart rate called reflex bradycardia (meaning slow heart). Therefore, the cursed victim is not really frightened to death; rather, a deathlike state comes when the sympathetic ANS ultimately turns off, and there is a rebound of equal and opposite magnitude by the parasympathetic ANS. As the parasympathetic system controls more and more of the victim's bodily functions, heart rate slows way down, and the person will slowly lose consciousness. In this state, the unlucky victim of the voodoo curse might appear to be dead. According to legend, some victims have even been buried while still alive, leading to fairly common myths about the dead rising from their graves, not looking too well, and certainly annoyed by the ugliness that was just perpetrated upon them—obviously, the makings of a great horror movie and everlasting legend.

Fortunately, there is some fascinating pharmacology to take from the voodoo death legends. Most legends talk about a zombie cucumber that was a potion containing extracts from the jimson weed, *Datura stramonium*, which would contain scopolamine. How would scopolamine help the victim of a zombie curse? Scopolamine would reduce the influence of the parasympathetic nervous system and prevent the victim from slipping into a zombie-like state.

The actions of scopolamine in the brain are rather complex. For example, low doses produce amnesia and activation of the sympathetic nervous system. They also can produce an array of peripheral side effects that are nicely exemplified by the following story published in 1980. Police in New York City were finding men wandering around the Central Park area without their pants and their wallets and with no idea what had happened to them during the previous few hours. The men could see and hear normally and safely avoid objects such as moving cars, dogs, and puzzled tourists. Their mouths were quite dry, and they had dilated pupils and very full bladders that they could not empty. These are all the symptoms of scopolamine ingestion. Ultimately, it was discovered that the men had recently visited prostitutes in the area and had been given a drink containing scopolamine, which had been stolen from a local pharmacy.

Higher doses of scopolamine, on the other hand, can produce visual and auditory hallucinations. The original witches flying ointment, so called because of its reputed use by medieval witches, was probably an herbal recipe that contained extracts from the *Datura* and *Mandragora* plants, as well as poplar leaves and fireplace soot, all of which were held together with animal fat or clove oil. In a ritual performed in the nude, the witches would rub the ointment on their foreheads, wrists, hands, or feet. According to Abramelin the Mage (1362–1460), a Jew from

Wurzburg, Germany, who wrote a series of books on magic and the occult, the women would also "anoint a staff and ride on it.or anoint themselves under the arms and in other hairy places." Their experiences may underlie the origination of stories about witches flying on broomsticks. By anointing "a staff" with the ointment and then riding on it naked, they would inevitably rub the ointment into the mucous membrane of their labia, which would ensure a speedy absorption of the lipid-soluble active ingredients of the plants in the ointment. The sensation produced by sufficient doses of these plant extracts would include both visual hallucinations and a floating, light-headed feeling; it's not hard to appreciate why these women might have reported an experience similar to flying through the sky while straddling their broomsticks.

These women likely had one thing in common with the Central Park men: they were effectively high on scopolamine. Although no one knows just how scopolamine is able to produce its complex psychoactive effects, those effects are clearly influenced by the dose of scopolamine consumed and by the number and location of muscarinic receptors within the brain that are antagonized. Ophthalmologists use scopolamine for clinical purposes—as an antagonist to block the muscarinic receptors expressed on the smooth muscles that encircle the iris of the eye and to allow the pupils to dilate, thus enabling these doctors to examine the interior of a patient's eyes. There may be another benefit as well, if the patient could see well enough to take advantage of it upon leaving the examination room: Those dilated pupils, unconsciously interpreted to indicate excitement, can be a real turn-on to other people. Indeed, people tend to rate others with dilated pupils as being more attractive and interesting. Von Linné knew this when he gave the species name of "belladonna," or beautiful woman, to one of the plants that produce scopolamine. Even today, products containing extracts of the *Atropa belladonna* plant are sold to women who want to be seen as beautiful and who use these extracts to dilate their eyes. Unfortunately, pupil dilation impairs vision and makes the user quite photophobic; it can also cause profound amnesia. Taken together, however, these multiple conditions might be seen as advantageous by a less attractive suitor.

ENHANCING ACETYLCHOLINE: NUT AND A MUSHROOM

Let's now turn away from the actions of drugs that are antagonists at the muscarinic acetylcholine receptors to consider drugs that are agonists (i.e., stimulants) at this receptor. Arecoline is one such agonist, found in the nut of the areca palm tree (*Areca catechu*) of Asia. The nut is used as mild euphoriant and antitussive (cough suppressant) throughout Southeast Asia. These effects indicate that arecoline is probably, at the very least, effectively stimulating the muscarinic acetylcholine receptors within the limbic (emotional) system and coughing centers of the brain.

The nut is often eaten wrapped in a leaf from the betel pepper tree (*Piper betle*), *together* with a piece of limestone; the presence of this bicarbonate-releasing stone increases the pH in the mouth and accelerates the absorption of arecoline and guva-coline from the nut. Some component of the nut is also con-verted into a bright red pigment that makes saliva become red and stains the teeth. After you've eaten this nut, your body con-verts some of it into a drug called guvacine, which is a potent enhancer of the neurotransmitter γ-aminobutyric acid (GABA), the brain's principal inhibitory transmitter molecule. Therefore, the twofold effect of consuming the Betel nut would be an enhance-ment of the inhibitory action of GABA throughout the brain (*see* later discussion in Chapter 6C) that is similar to that produced by a barbiturate or alcohol, as well as the stimulation of the acetyl-choline receptor. For reasons that are not well-understood, these combined effects produce feelings of happiness and well-being. These pleasurable feelings are probably the basis for nut's popu-larity in Southeast Asia.

Feelings of happiness and well-being can be produced by another drug, muscarine, which also acts by stimulating acetyl-choline receptors in the brain and body. Muscarine is present in the mushroom *Amanita muscaria*, which is very brightly colored and appears to be dotted with cottage cheese on its surface (Fig. 2–5). Eating this mushroom can also produce hallucina-tions, although its actual hallucinogenic constituent has not yet been conclusively determined. A typical hallucinogenic dose is about one to third dried mushrooms, depending on their size and growing conditions. The hallucinations are quite interest-ing. People report that normal objects appear bigger or smaller than they truly are; this is called macropsia or micropsia, respec-tively. The author Lewis Carroll was clearly aware of the perceptual

Figure 2–5. The *Amanita muscaria* mushroom.

changes produced by eating this mushroom, having incorporated them into his book, *Alice in Wonderland.* Carroll may have
become familiar with these mushrooms via his close friendship
with the famous mycologist (someone who studies fungi),
Mordecai Cooke.

The mushrooms also cause sleepiness and then delirium, so
at the very least, they probably interfere with the function of
acetylcholine neurons within the cortex. Upon waking, people
claim to feel very excited and aggressive for three to 4 hours and to
be able to perform extraordinary physical feats. These symptoms

are consistent with an overactive sympathetic nervous system. Why? Because the sympathetic nervous system, reduced in activity while the contents of the mushroom are in the body, rebounds in activity after the drug is excreted.

Petroglyphs found in 1968 in North Africa suggest the existence of a 12,000-year-old cult that is thought to have used the *Amanita muscaria* mushroom in religious rituals. The Amanita mushroom was also a popular recreational and ritualistic drug among people living in northern Europe. But perhaps its most memorable use was by the Vikings, whose rather unpleasant behaviors during their invasion of Ireland in the 8th century CE were described as "berserksgang" in the Irish poem "Fury of the Norsemen." From this poem, which includes the phrase "O Lord Deliver Us," you can get a clear idea of what happens when the brain is exposed to the contents of the *Amanita muscaria* mushroom. Its psychoactive ingredients must be quite stable in the body and quite resistant to digestive enzymes because they can be isolated from urine and re-used! They will "last" through approximately four consecutive users, as long as those users do not mind drinking someone else's urine. Evidently, the Vikings did not mind.

The mushroom was also known as "fly agaric" because of its ability to attract and kill flies. Flies also have muscarinic acetylcholine receptors on their neurons; after they ingest parts of the mushroom, the overstimulation of these receptors is apparently sufficient to kill them. But even if they somehow survive that fate, they're likely still doomed because of the actions of the mushroom on their retinas, which contain muscarinic acetylcholine receptors as well. After dining on mushroom pieces, the flies may become so visually impaired as to be vulnerable to a carefully aimed boot.

NICOTINE

And what about substances that act as agonists at the nicotinic acetylcholine receptor? At least two may be found in a fruit in your local grocery store. The chemicals punicalin and punicalagin are contained in the rind of the pomegranate, *Punica granatum*; the level of these chemicals is quite high and toxic, although pomegranate seeds are of course safe to eat. Another nicotinic agonist, cytosine, is from a more obscure source. It is contained in the seeds of the mescal bean, *Sophora secundiflora*, which was discovered in Central America in archaeological sites dating to 8000 years ago. The seeds are roasted over a fire and chewed to produce stimulation. The Mescalero Indians also added the beans to beer, whereas the Kickapoo Indians mixed it with tobacco leaves; this mixture was then used to treat earaches.

But by far one of the best studied agonists of the nicotinic acetylcholine receptor is nicotine. It occurs in more than 64 species of plants around the world, including the well-known tobacco plant, which likely utilizes nicotine as a defense against insects that express nicotine receptors in their body and are therefore vulnerable to its toxicity.

Tobacco was first used to treat persistent headaches, colds, and abscesses or sores on the head. Tobacco enemas were used to treat flatulence, and even more surprising, the smoke was once inhaled deeply to lessen bad coughs. In 1560, Jean Nicot (then the French Ambassador to Portugal) sent some tobacco to Catherine de Medici, who was then queen to Henry II of France; she reported that it helped treat her migraines. The plant initially was given the title of *herbe sainte*, or holy plant, and then later was dubbed *Herba Regina, the queen's herb*. Nicot got the credit for the discovery and Von Linné named the genus *Nicotiana* in his honor. Despite all this royal glory, in the 1890s the U.S. pharmacopeia dropped nicotine from its list of useful therapeutic agents.

A cigarette made from tobacco will contain about 1 to 2 milligrams of nicotine. Because nicotine is quite volatile and heat labile, only about 20% of it is actually inhaled into the body. However, because of its exceptional lipid solubility, at least 90% of the inhaled nicotine is absorbed into the body. Nicotine can also be rapidly absorbed by the mouth or intact skin. Once the smoke is inhaled, absorption via the lungs and transport to the brain occurs within 2 to 7 seconds. This makes smoking tobacco as efficient as an intravenous injection in terms of getting nicotine to its site of action within the brain. This speed of entry into the body may also underlie why nicotine is so toxic. Sixty milligrams is considered a lethal dose for a human; death takes only a few minutes to occur and results from a loss of control of the nicotinic receptors on the dia-phragm muscles.

Nicotine affects cortical function in a complex dose-dependent fashion; low doses tend to activate the left hemisphere and produce mental stimulation and a feeling of arousal, whereas high doses tend to activate the right hemisphere more strongly and are associated with the sedative effects of nicotine. Therefore, when doing boring tasks, you could take a low dose of nicotine by, say, smoking one cigarette and could increase your subjective feelings of arousal and attention. In contrast, during anxious or stressful situations, you could take a high dose of nicotine by chain-smoking and may actually reduce your stress by activating the right hemisphere and producing a bit of sedation. These findings nicely demonstrate the competing roles of nicotine receptors in the two hemispheres and tell us something profound about how the two halves of the brain normally function to produce a balance of emotions, attention, and arousal. Moreover, 60% of adults diagnosed with attention deficit disorder smoke cigarettes as compared to less than 30% of the rest of the population, another interesting finding that indicates that acetylcholine nicotinic receptors play an important role in paying attention.

Why is smoking so difficult to give up? Because ultimately it is so rewarding. Nicotine is the most addictive drug currently used by humans. It produces a dose-related euphoria that is most pronounced following overnight abstinence. Essentially, it provides its greatest pleasure with its first use of each day and re-addicts the user every morning. This may explain why heavy smokers enjoy lighting up as soon as they awaken in the morning. This is a common response of the brain to the absence of various chemicals that we consume; the re-introduction of a drug or nutrient after a prolonged delay produces a bigger effect. For example, food always tastes better when we're hungry. The sensitivity of the sensory neurons in our taste buds on the tongue is increased by hunger. Thus, if you're not a good cook, make your dinner guests wait an extra long time before serving the meal—your cooking will taste better to them. But if you're a dreadful cook, encourage your guests to smoke—this will tend to deaden their tastes buds.

After their initial morning smoke, and throughout the rest of the day, smokers carefully, and probably unconsciously, control the amount of nicotine that reaches their brain by altering the number of cigarettes they use per hour, the rate at which they take a puff, and the volume of their inhalation. This careful regulation may optimize the amount of acetylcholine nicotinic receptor stimulation and the balance of right versus left cortical activation to balance the level of stimulation and sedation. People with serious mental illness often are heavy smokers. They may be using nicotine to balance the activity between their two hemispheres and thereby lessen the severity of their symptoms. This potentially positive aspect of smoking may underlie why in 1948 the *Journal of the American Medical Association* stated that "from a psychological point of view, in all probability more can be said in behalf of smoking as a form of escape from tension than against it."

Today, our perception of nicotine has been altered principally by the consequences of the "vehicle" for nicotine administration, the tobacco plant. In the United States alone, tobacco use causes almost one death every minute, or the equivalent of four major airline crashes daily, similarly to what occurred on September 11, 2001. If we had to witness that tragedy every day, just imagine the public outcry for greater federal control of tobacco. Sadly, because of politics and the fact that tobacco sales (and their taxes) are such a boon to the U.S. economy, this is not likely to ever occur to such a degree as to ban these sales completely. Meanwhile, people will continue to die from tobacco use and will do so one at a time at home or in a hospital room, not in large groups on the evening news.

SUMMARY

The function of acetylcholine in our brain is determined by the brain regions that it influences; this is true for all of the neurotransmitters. Thus, acetylcholine neurons project into the frontal lobes and hippocampus; they therefore control our ability to pay attention, form new memories, or make decisions about our behavior. Drugs that antagonize acetylcholine, such as scopolamine, impair our ability to pay attention, make new memories, and control our behaviors. Drugs that enhance the function of acetylcholine by blocking its enzymatic destruction (e.g., physostigmine) in these brain regions tend to enhance our learning and memory ability. However, enhancing acetylcholine function too much can produce lethal effects, as in the case of nerve gases. Other drugs with the ability to manipulate acetyl-choline include those that, by blocking some muscarinic acetyl-choline receptors in the brain, produce hallucinations that once convinced women that they were flying. In contrast are drugs that are potent stimulants of the nicotinic subtype of acetylcho-line receptor. One such drug, nicotine, is so powerfully addict-ing that it induced our species to devote a significant portion of our farmland and economic resources to its continued survival on the planet.

The list of brain processes that are controlled by acetylcho-line and that are affected when it is blocked or stimulated seems lengthy because the neurons that release it project so broadly. However, manipulating acetylcholine function with drugs does not produce quite the dramatic effects on one brain process—mood regulation—that occur with the manipulation of some other neurotransmitter systems. As we will see in Chapter 3, the effects of certain drugs indicate that two neurotransmitters in particular play a far more critical role in the control of our moods.

Euphoria, Depression, & Madness

C an the function of just one small group of chemicals really determine whether you are happy or sad? The two neurotransmitters that are considered in this chapter, dopamine and norepinephrine, are chemicals called catecholamines that may do exactly that and much more. Catecholamines occur extensively throughout nature and have been identified in insects, crustaceans, arachnids (spiders), and primates. We know a lot about these neurotransmitters in the human brain primarily because so many drugs and nutrients have been discovered that can modify their function. This chapter looks at some of these substances and examines what their actions tell us about the function of these neurotransmitters. A consistent pattern of effects emerges: norepinephrine underlies the major components of arousal and behaviors that arise in association with increased arousal; dopamine is intimately related to the experience of reward and reward-seeking behaviors. Interestingly, it is also tied into the treatment of—if not directly implicated in the cause of—psychosis.

BASIC NEUROSCIENCE FOR NOREPINEPHRINE AND DOPAMINE

In humans, almost all of the norepinephrine neurons are located within a region called the locus coeruleus (Latin for "blue area") at the base of the brain. The name of this region is related to the fact that these neurons concentrate copper. Although copper is required for the synthesis of norepinephrine, the concentration of the copper far exceeds what is necessary for neurotransmitter synthesis. Unfortunately, the presence of this metal makes these neurons vulnerable to oxygen, which poses a particular risk for the brain. More on this point shortly, as well as in Chapter 9, but suffice it to say now that the act of breathing oxygen is a mixed blessing for those of us on the planet who have to do it for a living.

The norepinephrine neurons living in your locus coeruleus project throughout your brain. This broad access allows them to influence your level of arousal and thus almost every aspect of your thinking and behavior. Consistent with this role, it has recently been discovered that schizophrenic patients who display a chronic state of hyperarousal have significantly more norepinephrine neurons in their brains.

Although five times more in number than norepinephrine neurons, dopamine neurons do not project as widely throughout your brain. Instead, these neurons, which originate in a region called the midbrain, send projections forward primarily into basal ganglia and frontal lobes. One major dopamine pathway originates within the substantia nigra, or dark substance, so called because this region concentrates the metal iron into a pigmented substance known as melanin. As with the copper in the locus coeruleus, the oxidation of iron (you know this process as rusting) contributes a significant degree of neuronal vulnerability to oxygen. Indeed, many parts of your brain are actually rusting as you breathe. Recent evidence suggests that exposure to common pesticides and insecticides may also accelerate the process of cell death in the substantia nigra. The degeneration of the dopamine neurons in the substantia nigra underlies the progression and symptoms of Parkinson's disease, a disorder characterized by tremors, spasticity, and akinesia or the absence of movement. These symptoms provide insight into at least one major function of dopamine within your brain. The constant supply of dopamine is necessary to allow you to initiate or inhibit a movement. As you might expect, drugs that interfere with dopamine's normal function (e.g., some antipsychotic medications) produce side effects that resemble those seen in people with Parkinson's disease.

Another pair of dopamine pathways originates in a region of the midbrain near the substantia nigra and ascends upward into the brain. One pathway projects to brain regions that are associated with the control of emotion. The other dopamine pathway projects to the frontal lobes. For more than 50 years, scientists have speculated that excessive activity in these two pathways may underlie some of the symptoms associated with psychosis. We return to the potential role of dopamine in psychosis later.

The production of dopamine and norepinephrine in your brain begins with the amino acid tyrosine, which is obtained from your diet. Tyrosine is converted to the amino acid levodopa, or L-DOPA, by the enzyme tyrosine hydroxylase. One very important cofactor is iron. Without iron, tyrosine hydroxylase fails to function normally. People with anemia have reduced body levels of iron and, as consequently, may have reduced tyrosine hydroxylase activity and thus reduced production of norepinephrine and dopamine. The decreased brain levels of these important neurotransmitters may lead to a slight depression, although most likely only in people with severe anemia. Generally, in a normal healthy person, the production of these two neurotransmitters is not easily affected by the contents of the diet.

Tyrosine can also be acted on by the enzyme tyrosinase and converted into a dark pigment. This enzyme is quite interesting to study because it is vulnerable to a genetic mutation that makes it heat labile (i.e., it only works correctly in the cooler areas of the body). The consequence of this mutation is a lack of pigmentation in humans (albinism) and, conversely, the characteristic pattern of dark pigmentation at the ends of the nose, tail, ears, and paws of Siamese cats (i.e., those parts of the cat that are most distant from their warmer body core). Apparently, this enzyme is critical for the normal decussation, or crossing, of visual tracts, which also underlies the cross-eyed visual problems experienced by Siamese cats. I would suggest that the consequences of this mutation underlie this breed's peculiar personality as well.

The second critical enzymatic step in this pathway is the conversion of L-DOPA into dopamine. This conversion process is extremely efficient, which may explain why brain levels of L-DOPA tend to be very low and why providing exogenous L-DOPA to patients who lack sufficient dopamine—that is, those with Parkinson's disease—leads to a dramatic increase in the production of dopamine. The surviving dopamine neurons in these patients' brains will quickly convert L-DOPA into additional dopamine, which is then released.

There is a third enzyme expressed in norepinephrine neurons that converts dopamine into more norepinephrine; therefore, this enzyme is not expressed by dopamine neurons. The enzyme is stored within the synaptic vesicles and lies in wait for the entry of dopamine molecules once they have been synthesized in the cytoplasm of the neuron. In addition to this third enzyme, the vesicles contain copper and the anti-oxidant ascorbic acid, also known as Vitamin C. Copper is required for the enzyme to function appropriately. The ascorbic acid maintains the integrity of norepinephrine within the vesicle in the same way that ascorbic acid added to processed meats such as hotdogs lengthens the shelf life of these products. Neurons require anti-oxidants such as Vitamin C because they are continually exposed to oxygen from the blood. Without Vitamin C, many different neurotransmitters oxidize and become inactive while in storage in the vesicles.

All of these energy-demanding enzymatic steps are conducted for the single purpose of ensuring that your vesicles contain an adequate number of biologically active neurotransmitter molecules (usually about 10,000) when they release their contents into the synaptic space between neurons. This is the principal mechanism by which one neuron communicates with the next neuron. What would happen if the vesicles contained no neurotransmitter? Consider the effects of reserpine, a drug that is found in the snake root plant (*Rauwolfia serpentine*), which is indigenous to India, Pakistan, Sri Lanka, and Thailand. It prevents the transport of neurotransmitters into the vesicles for storage. If neurotransmitters cannot be stored safely in vesicles, then they are trapped in the cytoplasm, where they will be destroyed. When too many of the vesicles in nerve terminals are empty, it becomes much harder for your neurons to communicate with each other and nervous activity slows down. Therefore, at low doses, reserpine has a tranquilizing effect. At higher doses, because of the greatly reduced availability of these neurotransmitters, reserpine causes severe depression and mood shifts of the sort that might clarify why the snake root plant is called the insanity herb or "pagla-kadawa" by local Sherpas. The behavioral symptoms are caused by the deficiency of dopamine and norepinephrine, as well as of the neurotransmitter serotonin (*see* Chapter 4), and thus offer insight into the role that these neurotransmitters play in the control of arousal and mood. Given this insight, the effects of drugs that enhance the function of dopamine and norepinephrine in your brain should be easy to predict—that is, increased arousal and enhanced mood associated with euphoria. Let's now examine a few of these drugs.

THE AMPHETAMINES AND ECSTASY

The stimulant drug amphetamine dramatically and rapidly induces the release of norepinephrine and dopamine (and serotonin) into the synapse and greatly slows their inactivation by blocking reuptake back into the neuron. The increased and prolonged presence of these neurotransmitters within the synapse produces heightened alertness, euphoria, lowered fatigue, decreased boredom, depressed appetite, and insomnia. Once amphetamine leaves the brain, the rebound symptoms are extreme fatigue and depression.

During World War II, soldiers and airmen on both sides of the battle lines used amphetamine to combat boredom, fear, and fatigue and to increase endurance. Historians suggest that at end of the war, Adolf Hitler's increasingly paranoid behaviors may have resulted from his excessive use of amphetamines. Indeed, excessive and prolonged use of amphetamine can produce a condition similar to paranoid schizophrenia, and scientists once believed that studying the consequences of high doses of amphetamine would shed light on the causes of, and potential treatment for, psychosis.

More than half a century later, amphetamines are still popular in the world. However, because of our improved understanding of brain function and advances in medicinal chemistry, faster-acting and more potent versions of amphetamine have been invented. How? By making amphetamine more fat-soluble. As described in Chapter 1, one of the basic principles of neuropharmacology is that lipid (fat)-solubility is directly correlated with the speed of uptake of a drug into the brain. Furthermore, the faster a drug enters the brain, and somehow alters its physiology, the greater the euphoria the drug is likely to induce. This principle has been known to drug designers for many years. Morphine, for example, became far more lipid-soluble and far more euphoragenic (i.e., pleasure-inducing) when scientists added two acetyl groups to it to produce heroin at the turn of the 19th century. Much later, amphetamine was similarly modified to make it more euphoragenic and therefore more addicting. The simplest manipulation was the addition of a methyl group to make methamphetamine, which is a very potent relative of amphetamine that is far more lipid-soluble. Not surprisingly, its street name became "speed" because of its speedy entry into the brain.

Over time, attempts to make amphetamine ever more lipid soluble by the addition of carbon atoms (e.g., in the form of methyl or ethyl groups) has produced drugs that are more euphoragenic and hallucinogenic than amphetamine. The most famous of these is 3,4-methylene-dioxymethamphetamine, which is widely known as ecstasy. The action of ecstasy in the brain is very similar to amphetamine; it blocks the reuptake of dopamine, norepinephrine, and serotonin and enhances the release of these neurotransmitters. It also produces a dramatic rise in body temperature, or hyperthermia. Indeed, if you were to overdose on ecstasy, hyperthermia would be the cause of your death. How does this happen? Ecstasy has the ability to uncouple the energy-producing capacity of all of the mitochondria in your body. Uncoupling means that mitochondria lose their ability to generate ATP, which is your body's principal energy currency. When they cannot generate ATP, they start wasting their energy as heat. At typical doses of ecstasy, this uncoupling effect is seen most dramatically in the muscles. Because males have more muscle mass than females, on average, males are more sensitive to the acute toxic effects of the hyperthermia.

I've been amazed at the continued popularity of this drug among my students, who seem to believe that because they are young they are also immortal and therefore immune to the danger. I blame the feelings of immortality on the fact that their frontal lobes are not fully working because they have not yet completed the process of neuronal myelination. Without myelination, electrical signals from neurons fail to reach their destination. The parts of our brains that myelinate last are also the parts that evolved most recently. These parts include our frontal lobes, which contribute most to our unique personalities and allow us to anticipate the consequences of our actions.

Essentially, your frontal lobes tell you that it's a bad idea to drink alcohol and drive or to ignore the consequences of taking ecstasy. When your frontal lobes finally complete their process of myelination, they begin to work properly and you stop doing stupid things. Most importantly, you stop feeling immortal. Apparently, women finish this process by age 25 years and men finish by age 30. Thus a 20-year-old female, although her brain is still myelinating, is closer to maturity than her 20-year-old boyfriend, who still has another 10 years before he can really hear the sense of warnings such as those against drinking and driving or against taking any drug that comes his way. This delay in brain maturation among males may explain the behavior of many members of college fraternities.

MOTHER NATURE'S AMPHETAMINES

Amphetamine does not occur naturally, but some substances found in nature are chemically related to amphetamine and have similar effects on the brain. Ephedrine can be found in *Ephedra sinica*, which has been used in traditional Chinese medicine and is known as *ma huang*. Its effects on the sympathetic nervous system are similar to amphetamine. However, this extract never achieved complete success as a psychoactive stimulant, primarily because it does not cross the blood–brain barrier as effectively as amphetamine.

Khat is found in an African plant, *Catha edulis*, which contains cathinone and cathine (also known as d-norisoephedrine). The habit of chewing khat to produce a mild arousal probably predates coffee-drinking by centuries. Decoctions of the khat plant in hot water were once known as Abyssinian tea. As is true for most plant-derived biologically active drugs, the relative concentration of khat's active ingredients depends on where the plant is grown, its age, and the time elapsed after it was harvested. Cathinone is quite unstable, a property that makes storage for widespread distribution of the khat plant nearly impossible. You can, of course, purchase dried leaves from this plant in health food stores, but they do not contain any active ingredients. Other compounds in this plant, as in so many others, include chemicals called flavonoids that have anti-inflammatory properties. A few of the 40 different biologically active components of the khat plant also produce the unwanted side effects of green teeth and constipation. Because of the prevalence of this last side effect, the sale of laxatives is quite profitable in countries where khat is widely used.

Another naturally occurring drug that is similar to amphetamine can be found in the cactus *Lophophora williamsii*. Extracts are used to prepare a drink called peyote that contains 3,4,5-trimethoxyphenyl-ethylamine (the "meth" and "phenyl" point to a molecule that is quite lipid soluble). Known as mescaline, this compound is structurally similar to the catecholamines dopamine and norepinephrine but seems to act more directly upon serotonin receptors because of the presence of the methoxy groups on the molecule. This feature of the compound's structure would make the compound more fat-soluble and therefore better able to enter the brain quickly and may explain why mescaline produces an amphetamine-like euphoria at low doses and hallucinations at higher doses. Indeed, this euphoria-to-hallucination transition is a common dose-dependent characteristic of many psychoactive plant extracts.

Mescaline is either poorly metabolized or not metabolized at all by humans. Therefore, various and rather rigid cultural rituals developed a "recycling" program for the experience of ingesting it. Often, persons of highest social or religious rank would consume mescaline in large quantities, eventually passing it in their urine, which was then consumed by those of lesser social status. Sometimes, because of the gradual loss of potency, the urine from a few people needed to be combined to achieve the greatly anticipated experience. The Vikings were thus not the only group of ancient peoples willing to drink someone else's urine for a good time.

This reminds me of one of my students, a young woman, who claimed that her boyfriend liked to cook sections of this cactus into a lasagna-like preparation that he layered with ricotta cheese and tomatoes. She was curious whether the mescaline in his urine would remain active if she saved the urine for later use. Once you get past the obvious concerns about the sterility and purity of the collected urine (and the disturbing mental imagery), the active ingredient would probably be quite stable if stored frozen in orange or grapefruit juice to lower the pH of the urine. This approach would, as she observed, avoid the nasty gastrointestinal side effects that usually accompany eating this cactus because of the presence of non-psychoactive compounds that affect the gut's dopamine and serotonin neurons.

The drug asarone, which comes from a plant, *Acorus calamus* (found in Asia, Europe, and North America) is chemically very similar to mescaline. The roots of this plant are chewed to produce a dose-dependent effect; about 2 inches produces a mild euphoria, whereas nearly 10 inches produces hallucinations. In some cultures, wives will chew on the roots and collect their expectorant throughout the day for their husbands to enjoy later. Nothing says "welcome home" at the end of a hard day like a nice warm bowl of spit.

Various psychoactive spices have also been discovered that alter the function of the brain's dopamine, norepinephrine, and serotonin neurons. For example, the spice nutmeg comes from nutmeg tree, *Myristica fragrans*, and contains myristicin, which is also chemically quite similar to mescaline. (Myristicin is found in parsley and carrots as well but at very low concentrations.) Typically, one must consume about 30 grams of nutmeg powder—or roughly the contents of an entire container of the product that you could purchase at your local grocery store—to experience its psychoactive effects. Reactions vary considerably, from nothing at all, to euphoria at low doses, to marijuana- and D-lysergic acid diethylamide (LSD)-like experiences at higher doses, with hallucinations that can last up to 48 hours. Chronic use of high doses of nutmeg can produce a reaction similar to psychosis. One other unpleasant side effect of nutmeg is extreme diarrhea caused by the stimulation of dopamine and serotonin neurons within the gut. It has been claimed to be an aphrodisiac. Perhaps for that reason, one of my students consumed an entire canister of nutmeg that he had dissolved in some applesauce; the weekend he spent in the bathroom demonstrated why most people never try nutmeg more than once.

Spices such as saffron, fennel, dill, cinnamon, and anise also contain psychoactive substances that are chemically similar to myristicin. Generally, the level of psychoactive agents in these other spices is far too low to produce any noticeable consequences in people using them for cooking, but their role, regardless of how subtle, in enhancing the culinary experience should not be ignored.

Similar amphetamine-like substances have been found in kava kava, a drink prepared from roots of a pepper tree, *Piper methysticum,* which grows in the South Pacific islands. Piper is Latin for "pepper"; methysticum is Greek for "intoxicating." The drink contains various potentially psychoactive resins that include kawain, dihydrokawain, methysticin, dihydromethysticin, and yangonin. As is true for the complex ingredients of most plants, the psychoactive efficacy of the kava extract does not arise from any one of these compounds but rather from a blending of their effects in the brain. These resins are capable of stimulating dopamine and GABA receptors, and so their actions are similar to the effects of amphetamine and to some popular anti-anxiety drugs (discussed in Chapter 6). The resins from this plant are quite fat-soluble and thus will enter the brain relatively easily and quickly to produce a relaxed euphoria and sometimes, at high doses, hallucinations.

It is possible to go into many upscale grocery stores and purchase extracts of kava kava plants, but their ingredients are no longer active. Real kava kava tends to be unstable, particularly with the liquid storage that is commonly used in these products. Given the unstable nature of the ingredients of this plant, the presumed anti-anxiety actions of kava kava extracts obtained in U.S. stores results entirely from the placebo effect (*see* Chapter 9).

COCAINE

The comedian Robin Williams once quipped that cocaine is God's way of telling you that you're making too much money. The United States must indeed be a wealthy country, considering that 3 million of our fellow citizens abuse this drug; this is six times the number of heroin addicts in our nation. It is estimated that 50% of Americans between the ages of 25 and 30 years has tried cocaine.

What does cocaine do in the brain? First, it binds to sodium ion channels and blocks them from functioning. This action stops the flow of action potentials and prevents neurons from communicating with each other. Cocaine also blocks the conduction of pain signals, which explains why, after it was isolated from the coca plant (*Erythroxylon coca*) in 1855, it was used as a local anesthetic, including for the eye and for toothaches. But ultimately, its anesthetic actions would be discovered to have nothing to do with the reason for its later illegal street use: its ability to produce euphoria.

Cocaine acts similarly to amphetamine with regard to its ability to enhance the effects of the catecholamines and serotonin at the synapse. The actions of cocaine on the brain lead to increased alertness, reduced hunger, increased physical and mental endurance, increased motor activity, and an intensification of most normal pleasures. This last feature may explain why so many claim that cocaine enhances emotional and sexual feelings. Cocaine abusers usually co-administer other drugs that are brain depressants (e.g., alcohol, heroin, or marijuana) to decrease the unpleasant hyperstimulant aspects of cocaine.

Approximately 16 to 32 milligrams of cocaine is an effective street dosage that is usually without immediate negative side effects. An increase in heart rate usually occurs within about 8 minutes after administration and dissipates 30 to 40 minutes later. The half-life, or the time it takes for half of the drug to exit the blood and body, is about 40 to 50 minutes. Cocaine will actually degrade spontaneously in the body to produce an inactive compound with a tongue-twister name, benzoylecgonine. The physiological effects of cocaine are therefore much shorter than those of amphetamine. Partly for this reason, most users claim that it does not "wear out" the body in the same way that amphetamine does.

Getting cocaine to its site of action within the brain first requires getting adequate amounts of the drug into the blood. Snuffing cocaine by applying it to mucous membranes inside the nose is much more effective than either oral administration or intravenous use because the drug enters the blood and brain more quickly and is therefore more immediately euphoragenic. Unfortunately, there is a problem with this approach to getting cocaine into the blood. Cocaine constricts the blood vessels feeding the cartilage in the bridge of the nose and, with repeated nasal application, leads to the ischemic (lack of blood) death of the tissues supporting the end of the nose. Initially, the irritation to the tissue causes a runny nose; ultimately, the irritation leads to a true necrosis, or cell death, and the end of the nose either collapses or becomes quite distorted.

Orally administered cocaine is not well-absorbed from gastrointestinal tract, and its effects on the brain thus tend to be far less reinforcing when taken in this fashion. However, oral administration does have a long history. Many years before cocaine extracts were applied to mucous membranes, ancient peoples simply ate the leaves of the coca plant. Indeed, although cocaine use peaked in the 1880s and the 1980s, chewing coca leaves for their psychoactive effects—they contain up to 1% of cocaine by weight—was certainly a popular practice long before these eras. The leaves have been found in 5000-year-old graves. Approximately 800 years ago in South America, people started chewing the leaves wrapped around a piece of limestone to increase the pH in their mouths and to augment the release of cocaine from the leaves. By improving the extraction of cocaine from the leaves, the experience became far more pleasurable. The Incas introduced religious ritual to its use and invented the word "cocata" to describe the distance a person could walk on one chew of coca leaf before the beneficial effects wore off. The tribal chiefs gave coca leaves to runners in the Andes Mountains to help them tolerate the altitude and to increase their endurance; the runners were also paid in coca leaves, thus maintaining their addiction and continued service until they died of exhaustion and malnutrition. The conquering Spanish subsequently recognized the cost-saving wisdom in this approach and paid their Incan servants with coca leaves, enabling them to work harder and eat less food. Amerigo Vespucci, who gave his name to the newly "discovered" land, wrote about the use of coca leaves by the local tribes.

Fast-forward a number of centuries, and we see the oral use of coca plant extracts taking a new form. In 1862, Angelo Mariani, a Corsican chemist, combined a Bordeaux wine with coca plant extracts to produce and sell *Vin Mariani*. The labels displayed testimonials from Pope Leo XIII, who gave it the Vatican's gold medal of appreciation, as well as from President Ulysses S. Grant and from Thomas Edison, who claimed that it helped him stay awake longer to complete his experiments. *Vin Mariani* was such a commercial success that many other alcohol-based tonics containing coca leaf extracts were introduced in the late 1880s. One quite successful tonic was introduced by John S. Pemberton in 1884. Pemberton called his drink "A French wine of coca, ideal tonic." Later, in 1886, he removed the alcohol, replaced cocaine with an extract from the kola nut, and called it *Coca-Cola*. But why combine coca leaf extracts with wine in the first place? The reason is that the combined effect of these two drugs on the brain is far more euphoragenic, and therefore more addicting, than either compound alone. When combined with alcohol, as in Vin Mariani, the mixture forms a powerful psychoactive compound called coca-ethylene, which is more lipid-soluble than cocaine and thus enters the brain faster; by now you know what that implies in terms of the enhanced pleasure it will produce.

Drug designers are never far behind the chemists in discovering new ways to make drugs enter the brain faster. After all, greater addiction of one's customers leads to higher profits! Thus, in the 1960s free-base cocaine was produced and people discovered that it very quickly entered the blood and brain and produced an ever greater euphoria. The natural product that had been obtained from the coca leaf for so many centuries exists as cocaine hydrochloride; this is an acidic compound that can be volatilized—that is, turned into a vapor. However, at a high temperature, the cocaine is destroyed. This is why naturally occurring cocaine was never smoked; the active ingredient is completely lost. I would predict that someone somewhere at some time must have tried smoking coca leaves and found that it was a disappointing failure. To be effective when smoked, cocaine must be reconverted chemically to its alkaloid or base form. The process of converting and then isolating the product is called free-basing. The conversion process requires the use of highly flammable solvents that when not properly handled can set celebrities (e.g., the comedian Richard Pryor) on fire.

More recently, modifications in the process of making the basic form of the drug have produced cocaine crystals that spontaneously generate small chunks; this product is called Crack—related to the sound the crystals make when heated. It can be smoked and, therefore, will deliver cocaine into the brain as fast as an intravenous injection, but without the inconvenient and potentially unhealthy process of using a needle.

Cocaine is so rewarding that its users prefer it to sex, food, and water, thus overriding basic survival drives. In experiments, laboratory animals will self-administer cocaine to the point of severe toxicity, physical exhaustion, and even death. Many human users support their habit by selling cocaine or by stealing from friends and coworkers. Even Sigmund Freud, who wrote a scholarly and quite accurate treatise on cocaine's effects in "Uber Coca" (1884), got carried away and claimed his use of the drug cured his morphine addiction. In fact, it simply became a second addiction for him.

The compelling and overwhelming nature of cocaine addiction is impressive and tells us something profound about how the brain is built. It is apparently comprised of critically important internal neural systems that can produce a powerful rewarding experience usually connected to activities that are the basis for the survival of our species: eating and reproduction. Drugs such as cocaine can hijack these neural processes and stimulate the brain's reward centers so excessively and unnaturally that users will crave more stimulation, as they would normally crave food and sex. From the brain's perspective, there is no real difference between these cravings. Thus, the familiar moral fiber argument of "just say no" is unbelievably naïve, its application cruel. It ignores the complexities of the brain and the influence of culture and evolution on how the brain responds to drugs.

How precisely does cocaine achieve these effects in the brain? As described in Chapter 1, once a neurotransmitter is released from its neuronal terminal, its actions within the synapse are ended principally by reuptake into the presynaptic terminal. Cocaine primarily blocks the reuptake of dopamine but also acts similarly on norepinephrine and serotonin reuptake. If your neuronal terminals can be seen as acting like little vacuum cleaners, then cocaine essentially clogs the vacuum nozzle. As a consequence of this blockade, the concentrations of dopamine, norepinephrine, and serotonin within the synaptic cleft between two neurons increases dramatically. Within millions of synapses in the brain, these neurotransmitters are now free to continue to stimulate their receptors over and over, again and again. There are neuronal terminals for dopamine, norepinephrine, and serotonin scattered throughout the entire brain, and thus the consequences of cocaine on brain function are also widespread.

And as we've seen before, what happens after a drug exits the brain tells us something about what parts of the brain were affected under the influence of that drug. With regard to cocaine, these include the arousal systems within the brainstem, the feeding centers within the hypothalamus, and the reward centers within the frontal lobes and limbic system. Thus, cocaine reduces the need for sleep, and its absence produces extreme sleepiness; it reduces the desire to eat, and its absence is associated with increased food consumption; it produces extreme euphoria, and its absence leads to a severe depression (it is thought that the emotional highs and lows that cocaine abuse produces over time may explain the origin of the novella, *The Strange Case of Dr. Jekyll and Mr. Hyde,* by Robert Louis Stevenson). Excessive, long-term, intravenous use of cocaine tends to produce especially severe rebound phenomena, including psychotic behaviors together with delusions of grandeur and hallucinations. For many drugs that affect the brain, including cocaine, the degree of rebound symptoms is typically related to how many times a person has used the drug. Moreover, the effects of cocaine on brain chemistry and physiology may be long term. Even after they are withdrawn from the drug, most chronic users report visual disturbances such as "snow lights" and other sensory disturbances such as formication, or the feeling of bugs crawling on the skin; these symptoms usually only occur after prolonged use of cocaine. These delayed effects might be viewed as echoes of neural activity reverberating within the circuits of the brain following the powerful stimulation produced by the cocaine.

Lidocaine is chemically similar to cocaine; it is also a sodium channel-blocking drug, which is why it is an effective topical pain reliever that is commonly sold over the counter in drug stores. However, in contrast to cocaine, it has no reinforcing, euphoric effect at all, and animals, including humans, will not self-administer it. This confirms the validity of the finding that the anesthetic actions of cocaine do not contribute to its ability to produce euphoria.

But what does explain why we experience euphoria from cocaine or amphetamine or ecstasy? Euphoria is the brain's unfailing response to the fast entry of drugs that increase the level of the neurotransmitter dopamine in the synapse between neurons. Again, increasing the fat-solubility of these drugs speeds their entry into the brain and makes them more pleasurable. The brain behaves as though it likes drugs that quickly change its level of activity. Just how does dopamine facilitate this experience?

DOPAMINE: THE GAS PEDAL OF PLEASURE

Much of our current evidence provides only indirect confirmation of dopamine's role in experiencing pleasure. First, every drug of abuse somehow enhances the function of dopamine neurons. Probably everything we choose to do for pleasure, including eating or having sex or listening to beautiful music, somehow affects our dopamine neurons. Second, drugs that antagonize the function of dopamine, such as the antipsychotic drugs to be discussed in the next section, greatly reduce our ability to experience pleasure. Third, dopamine sets the pace at which the frontal lobes process information, akin to setting the ticking rate of a clock. The faster your clock ticks, the faster your brain processes information. Drugs that increase the release of dopamine often speed up your thinking process. They also produce increased motor activity, such as pacing and fidgeting. We see these side effects in children treated with drugs, all of which are chemically modified molecules of amphetamine, for attention deficit disorder; their performance in school improves but they are more hyperactive. Drugs such as amphetamine and cocaine speed up the clock, whereas drugs that impair the function of dopamine, such as the antipsychotics, tend to slow mental processing speed. With normal aging, the slow decline in the release of dopamine in the frontal lobes gradually slows one's ability to process information as quickly as one could when younger. Patients with Parkinson's disease, caused by the degeneration of dopamine neurons, suffer from the slowing of their higher cognitive abilities and from emotional depression, including the inability to experience pleasure. The drugs that patients with Parkinson's take to lessen their symptoms enhance the function of dopamine and tend to produce a slight euphoria and occasionally an increase in the incidence of compulsive behaviors such as gambling.

Considered together, the effects of a diverse array of drugs all signify that your brain is a racecar and that dopamine is the gas pedal. Your brain "feels" euphoria when the gas pedal is pushed quickly (by ever increasing lipid-solubility), and your thoughts are allowed to fly as fast as possible around your mental track. The forces of evolution have shaped your brain to truly enjoy working fast; the faster the better because fast brains are more likely to exist within creatures who survive and who will therefore pass on this trait to the next generation. Thus, classic Darwinism underlies why we enjoy what we enjoy so much, be it having sex, or eating chocolate or ingesting drugs of abuse like amphetamine, ecstasy, and cocaine.

TREATING PSYCHOSIS

What happens when the gas pedal is stuck full on? Is this the basis of psychosis? What can be done to fix it? Whatever the causes of psychosis may be, almost universally, the treatment is to block dopamine receptors. Most of the catecholamine-enhancing drugs that I've discussed thus far interfere with the ability of the brain's presynaptic neurons to produce, store, and release or inactivate the neurotransmitters dopamine and nor-epinephrine. Antipsychotic drugs, however, work at the other side of the synapse, achieving considerable therapeutic efficacy in many psychotic patients by blocking the function of their dopamine receptors in postsynaptic neurons. Let's now look at what this action can teach us about the function of dopamine in the brain and the neurological mechanisms underlying psychosis.

Psychosis is essentially a generic term for a mental condition associated with a loss of contact with reality. Individuals who are psychotic report hallucinations, delusions, and highly disorganized thinking. As a result, they tend to have great difficulty functioning in their daily lives and have trouble sustaining normal social interactions with others. Drugs that block dopamine receptors are capable of reducing some of the symptoms associated with psychosis. But herein lies a complexity—in no way do the antipsychotic effects of these drugs prove that psychosis is caused by a dysfunction of dopamine neurons, any more than reducing depressive symptoms in some people through medications that selectively block reuptake of dopamine, norepinephrine or serotonin proves that a dysfunction of these neurotransmitters underlies the depression. This is a very important general point to consider when examining drug action as a way of understanding brain function.

In fact, an alteration in dopamine function probably does not cause psychosis; rather, it is most likely just a secondary consequence of a complex array of alterations of one or more different neural systems in the brain. This may explain why the blockade of some dopamine receptors within certain brain regions reduces the severity of a few bothersome psychotic symptoms but not others. The antagonism of dopamine receptors may simply compensate for the presence of an error of chemistry that exists somewhere in the brain. Whatever the reason for their efficacy, all we know for certain is that antipsychotics that block dopamine receptors provide significant benefits for some, but not all, patients.

Unfortunately, these drugs—especially the "first generation" of antipsychotics introduced in the 1950s—have side effects similar to those seen in patients with Parkinson's disease: tremors when at rest, reduction of voluntary movement, muscle spasticity and dystonia, or sustained muscle contractions. These symptoms confirm the role of dopamine neurons in the initiation and control of movement. Antipsychotic drugs also block dopamine receptors within a region of the brain that controls the release of the hormone prolactin. The result is an increase in the release of prolactin and thus an increase in breast tissue growth. Increased breast development can be very disturbing to male patients who may already be paranoid regarding the medications they are prescribed.

Newer, "second generation" antipsychotics have side effects as well—for example, they may cause significant weight gain that many patients find frustrating. Recent evidence suggests that the weight gain is related to the blockade of histamine receptors in the brain. Interestingly, the original clinical use of the first antipsychotic drug, chlorpromazine (sold as Thorazine in the United States), occurred because of its ability to block histamine receptors and reduce symptoms of the common cold; only later was it recognized that this drug could also reduce psychotic symptoms. Recently, the connection between histamine and dopamine in the brain became even more interesting. Apparently many of the newer over-the-counter antihistamine medications are capable of the blocking reuptake of dopamine in a manner reminiscent of cocaine. Suddenly, treating one's sniffles has become a far more euphoragenic experience!

In a manner similar to that observed following treatment with antidepressant drugs, the side effects of dopamine receptor blockade occur rather quickly but the clinical benefits require 2 to 3 weeks, or more, to fully develop. This also implies that compensatory changes in brain function are required for these drugs to produce clinical benefits in psychotic patients. These changes most likely require the activation or inactivation of genes in a specific population of neurons within selected brain regions.

SUMMARY

Drugs that enhance the function of dopamine and norepinephrine (e.g., cocaine, mescaline, amphetamine, and its related chemicals such as ecstasy) produce a pleasurable feeling of euphoria and enhanced arousal; therefore, these drugs are heavily abused. If we look at the dopamine system in particular, we can see that it is designed to make us feel pleasure, an experience that reinforces our basic survival needs such as eating and having sex. Drugs that produce euphoria do so because they take advantage of and are reinforced by this reward system. By contrast, dysfunction of our dopamine system or ingestion of drugs that block dopamine (e.g., the antipsychotics) is famous for taking away our ability to experience pleasure. In addition, because of the presence of dopamine in our basal ganglia, blocking dopamine interferes with our ability to move our bodies smoothly and easily. Norepinephrine-containing neurons project very broadly and diffusely throughout the brain, giving a clue to its function as well. When drugs stimulate norepinephrine receptors, we experience a dose-dependent transition from simple arousal to a full-blown response associated with a rapidly beating heart and fast respiration. We become aroused and ready for either pleasure or pain: it does not matter which to our brain, the response is the same.

By now you have a sense of the interwoven roles of dopamine, norepinephrine, and acetylcholine in the control of movement, reward, mood, arousal, and learning and attention. By considering how various drugs manipulate these neurotransmitter systems within the brain, scientists have discovered some consistent patterns that allow us to make predictions about what to expect when specific types of drugs are taken. The same holds true for the neurotransmitter system mentioned several times in this chapter: serotonin. What are the consequences of its manipulation in the brain? Read on.

CHAPTER 4

———

YOUR BRAIN'S ANCHOR TO REALITY

How does the brain filter incoming sensory information so that sights and sounds do not become all mixed together? What happens when the brain loses this filtering ability as a result of, say, taking a hallucinogenic drug? What have we learned about depression and anxiety from the drugs that we administer to treat these disorders? The answers to these questions are slowly being revealed as more becomes known about the actions of serotonin in the brain.

Serotonin is a very ancient neurotransmitter and has been found in the venom of amphibians, wasps, and scorpions and within the nematocysts of the sea anemone as well as in the nervous system of parasitic flatworms, crickets, and lobsters. Within the human body, 90% of the total serotonin is contained within the neurons of the gut and is released from the intestines to determine bone growth or shrinkage. Another 8% of the body's serotonin is found in the blood and is localized inside platelets and mast cells; in fact, it was initially discovered in *serum* and determined to have *tonic* (or constricting) effects on the vascular system—hence its name. The remaining few percent is found in the brain, in roughly the same location as in every other vertebrate brain, leading scientists to conclude that this neurotransmitter system was present in the primitive nervous system at least one half-billion years ago.

THE POWER OF A FEW PERCENT

Neurons that produce and release serotonin in the brain are organized into a series of nuclei that lie in a chain along the midline, or seam, of the brainstem; these are called the raphe nuclei (raphe means seam in Latin). These neurons project their axons to every part of the brain, and some of these axons make contact with blood vessels; the neurons also project downward into the spinal cord. If you were able to insert a recording device into the major raphe nuclei and "listen" to the activity of your serotonin neurons, you would discover that they have a regular slow spontaneous level of activity that varies little while you are awake. When you fall asleep, the activity of these neurons slows. When you start to dream—or if, as we'll see shortly, you ingest a hallucinogen—these neurons cease their activity completely.

Despite the relative scarcity of serotonin in your brain, drugs that alter serotonin function can produce profound changes in how you feel and how you experience the world around you. For example, such drugs often stimulate the sympathetic autonomic nervous system and produce increased heart rate, increased respiration, dilated pupils, and other unpleasant side effects. On the other hand, the effects of serotonin upon blood vessel dilation may underlie the ability of an entire class of drugs, known as the tryptans, to attenuate the pain associated with a migraine headache. Other drugs can also help alleviate symptoms that often accompany migraines and that involve serotonin: depression and sleep problems.

The production of serotonin requires the absorption of the amino acid tryptophan from your food. Transport of this amino acid is influenced by the level of other amino acids in your blood; that level, in turn, is also influenced by what you eat. Within the neurons of your brain, tryptophan is converted to 5-hydroxy-tryptophan by tryptophan hydroxylase, an enzyme that is usually not saturated with substrate. Therefore, if you eat less tryptophan, your brain generally produces less serotonin. Conversely, providing additional tryptophan in the diet may lead to increased production of serotonin within neurons. It is worth noting, however, that simply producing more of any neurotransmitter does not guarantee that the neuron will actually release it. If too much serotonin is produced, then the excess is simply discarded. Studies have shown that only extreme depletion or supplementation of this amino acid in the diet can influence serotonin-controlled brain processes such as mood and sleep.

Moreover, the absence of the release of serotonin in the brain has been correlated with the initiation of hallucinations. This is not to say that we can manipulate our diet to so undermine serotonin release as to experience a hallucination. We cannot. But certain drugs that will initiate this effect, and their action, as well as the experiences they produce, can tell us something about the normal function of serotonin in the brain.

HALLUCINOGENS

How do hallucinogens work? One hallucinogenic drug, LSD, binds to a variety of different serotonin-sensitive receptors on the surface of serotonin neurons and slows their rate of firing. At the left side of Figure 4–1, you can see graphically what the activity of serotonin would look like if you placed an electrode into one of the raphe nuclei in the brainstem and then administered LSD to it. At first, the firing is quite regular. The arrow in the figure shows when LSD was injected into the brain. Only a few minutes later, you can see that the activity of the serotonin neurons slows way down, similarly to that seen when we enter dream sleep. But that similarity is only a neat coincidence; given that the psychoactive effect of LSD far outlasts the slowing of serotonin neural activity, this slowed activity does not explain completely why we hallucinate on this drug and why the hallucinations are so like dreaming. Indeed, the effects of LSD on serotonin neurons may only be the initial trigger that sets in motion a cascade of complex processes throughout the brain that is experienced as a hallucination.

A naturally occurring version of LSD is D-Lysergic acid monoethylamide. It is slightly less fat-soluble (one less ethyl group) than LSD, but it too can produce hallucinations. *Claviceps purpurea*, the ergot fungus that produces this compound, also generates a toxin that mimics the action of serotonin, particularly its ability to constrict blood vessels. Consumption of bread made from grain or corn that is contaminated with this fungus causes a burning in the extremities resulting from extreme constriction of blood vessels and leads to limb death. One outbreak of ergotism, as this condition came to be known, may have caused the death of nearly 40,000 people in Europe in 944 CE; at that time, it was called *ignis sacer*, or "Saint Anthony's holy fire," after the monks of the Order of St. Anthony. Consumption of ergot-contaminated grains may also have been responsible for a number of mystical experiences in the past, including the ancient Greek ceremonies known as the Eleusinian Mysteries. Some historians even believe that ergot-contaminated rye may

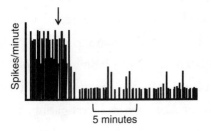

Figure 4–1. The activity of serotonin would look like this if you placed an electrode into one of the raphe nuclei in the brainstem. If LSD is administered at the arrow, then the activity of these cells slows down.

have caused the behaviors that eventually led to the Salem witch-craft trials that began in December of 1691. According to available records, eight girls suffered with "distempers" that included, according to witnesses, "disorderly speech, odd postures and gestures, and convulsive fits." Although ergotism was quite familiar to medical science and to historians by the 17th century, the New England puritans chose to see these symptoms as the work of Satan brought about by the practice of witchcraft. By September of 1692, 20 men and women were tried and executed for "their part" in the practice, and 2 died in prison.

Psilocybin, a chemically similar naturally occurring molecule, is much less potent than LSD but likely shares aspects of its actions on serotonin neurons once the body converts it into psilocin. Our ancestors probably discovered its source, *Psilocybe Mexicana, P. semilanceata, and P. cyanescens*, by accident when foraging for edible mushrooms. One can only imagine how unexpected the experience must have been for the first person who inadvertently prepared one of these mushrooms for consumption, bringing new meaning to the phrase "dinner and a show."

Sixteenth-century Central American Indians, according to the naturalist Francisco Hernandez, called them "*Teonanacatl*," possibly translated as "God's flesh" or, simply, "sacred mushroom." Albert Hofmann, the scientist credited with the inadvertent discovery of LSD when investigating its effects, is also credited with isolating the active ingredient of this mushroom in 1958. He claimed to have ingested 32 dried mushrooms, probably 10 times the usual dose taken today, to determine their effects and wrote that they were similar to those he had experienced with LSD.

Psilocybin can, in fact, be found in more than 75 different species of mushrooms. It is also chemically similar to bufotenine, an interesting hallucinogenic molecule that is chemically very similar in structure to serotonin. Bufotenine has been discovered in a truly diverse set of locations: the skin and glands of a South American toad, seed pods from the South American tree *Piptadenia peregrine,* and the leaves and bark of the Central American mimosa, *Acacia niopo.* The seeds from *Piptadenia peregrine* are ground with limestone to increase the extraction of the bufotenine, much as tobacco companies today add ammonia to raise the pH and increase the absorption of nicotine in your mouth. The grounded blend of bean pod and limestone is used as a snuff called "yopo." Young boys blow the snuff into each other's nostrils through a forked tube made from hollow chicken bones. Interestingly, bufotenine may also be present in the *Amanita muscaria* mushroom, which may be responsible for some of the psychoactive effects described in Chapter 2. The actions of bufotenine on the brain are still speculative because no one has yet demonstrated that it can actually cross the blood–brain barrier. Bufotenine's reputation may be more directly related to its toxic effects outside of the brain.

In fact, no one is currently certain how LSD or any of the hallucinogens actually works, or just how serotonin factors into their hallucinatory effects. Confounding this uncertainty is the fact that some hallucinogens have no apparent effect on serotonin at all. For example, Salvinorin A, from the Mexican plant *Salvia divinorum*, is a very potent naturally occurring hallucinogenic compound that is similar to morphine in its actions but has no identified action at serotonin receptors.

WHAT ARE HALLUCINATIONS?

The complex sensory experience known as hallucinations can, however, occur from other sources besides drugs like LSD or psilocybin, and this fact may shed some light on the nature of the hallucinatory experience, drug-induced or otherwise, and its connection to serotonin. Consider, for example, the following hypothetical scenario:

Imagine yourself as a newborn lying in a crib. Your brain's serotonin neurons at this age, and during the first couple years of your life, are not working completely because the neurons and glia that support them have not fully developed. In addition, the profile of serotonin receptors has not yet converted to the adult balance of excitatory and inhibitory subtypes of receptors. Your sensory systems—visual, auditory, and olfactory abilities in particular—are working, but your serotonergic system is not adequately installed to assist them with the processing of the incoming sensory information to the brain. Suddenly, you sense something looming over your crib—a large green, distorted face with a screeching voice and reeking of a yellow odor—and you scream in fear. You have just had your first hallucination. You have also just experienced synesthesia, or the merging and mixing of sensory processes—for example, sights that produce sounds or smells that have color.

Now imagine yourself 20 years later, with your serotonergic system now fully developed. Let's assume that you yourself are not actually a "synesthete," that rare person who has this condition as an inherited part of his or her life. But take a hallucinogenic drug at age 20 years (or any adult age), and you could have a temporary synesthetic experience similar to what you had in your crib as an infant. Why? The inhibited function of your serotonergic system that is induced by a hallucinogen may reproduce the condition of synesthesia that was simply "normal" when you were a newborn. As a newborn, you would find this condition to be frightening. But as an adult who has taken a hallucinogen, you might, in the right setting, come to believe that the condition is a transcendently mystical experience.

SEROTONIN AND RELIGIOSITY

Timothy Leary, the famous LSD guru of the 1960s counterculture movement, once commented in 1964, "A psychedelic experience is a journey to new realms of consciousness. The scope and content of the experience is limitless, but its characteristic features are the transcendence of verbal concepts, of space-time dimensions, and of the ego and identity." His description has a spiritual flavor that might be very familiar to people who are skillful at tantric yoga or transcendental meditation. Mind-altering or mind-expanding drugs, usually referring to hallucinogens, alter your consciousness, your sense of personal space and time, and your perception of the real world around you. In reality, the actions of hallucinogens in the brain that lead to an "expanding of the mind" probably result from relatively subtle alterations in normal serotonin neuronal function. These changes, as mentioned, set in motion a cascade of poorly understood neural processes that impair aspects of normal consciousness.

One function of consciousness, and a role probably influenced by serotonin, is to filter out the overwhelming and confusing mass of sensory input that your brain receives while you are awake. If you lose the ability to filter incoming sensory stimuli, you would probably become very disoriented and confused. Drug-induced mind expansion can therefore only be experienced safely—that is, so as to avoid completely freaking out, in a highly structured and protected setting. It should come as no surprise then that many cultures have developed strict religious and social rules around the use of plants that produce hallucinations. Extracts from psychoactive plants, or symbolic representations of them such as the burning of incense, have often played a significant role in religious ceremonies. Indeed, the near universal co-occurrence of religion and the use of natural hallucinatory agents may point to the crossroads that connect various hypotheses on why religiosity is so common across diverse primitive societies.

What I'm suggesting is that the appearance of the small mystical societies in ancient times that ultimately evolved into more familiar organized religions was assisted by the near universal presence of hallucinogenic plants that were able to alter how the brain functioned and to facilitate each culture's communication with their gods and goddesses. If true, then it should also come as no surprise that in recorded history, humans have worshiped more than 2500 major deities; the actual number is probably far greater. The similarities between a hallucinatory experience and, for some, an intense religious experience are consistent with the hypothesis that religion has a biological basis that was shaped by our shared evolution with, and constant exposure to, the hallucinatory plants around us. The widespread use of hallucinogenic plants by our ancestors may underlie some of the fantastic stories that have become associated with various religions. For example, some people believe that first chapter of the Book of Ezekiel describes this prophet's encounter with beings from outer space during the 6th century BCE; a more reasonable explanation might be that the experience was initiated by the consumption of an hallucinogenic plant targeting the brain's serotonergic system. Therefore, because serotonin neurons play a role in how hallucinogens interact with the brain, it is also possible that serotonin plays a role in the individual expressions of religiosity across cultures.

In addition, there may be a correlation between religiosity, specific genetic markers underlying the function of serotonin, and other mental experiences besides hallucinations. Genetically altered mice and positron emission tomography (PET) studies on humans have been very useful in demonstrating the potential role of specific serotonin receptors in the regulation of mood and anxiety. For example, mice lacking a particular serotonin receptor, known as type 5HT-1A, show more anxiety-like behavior. Some recently discovered drugs target this receptor to reduce the symptoms of depression and anxiety in humans. The overall effectiveness of these drugs at least suggests that this receptor in particular may play an important role in the normal control of anxiety or mood.

So what's the connection to one's personal degree of religiosity? The number of type 5HT-1A serotonin receptors in the brain is inversely correlated with self-ratings of religiosity and spirituality. People who respond negatively (e.g., with excessive anxiety or depression) to the challenges of everyday life have fewer 5HT-1A receptors and are more likely to find comfort in religious faith and practice. Moreover, a series of studies have demonstrated that people with certain serotonin receptor profiles suffer more often with social anxiety disorder, which is characterized by an extreme fear that other people are thinking bad things about them. Fortunately, these people also tend to respond more positively to placebos or affirmative suggestions than people who do not have these types of serotonin receptors in their brain. Taken together, these findings suggest that people who yearn for more religious leadership in their lives may have inherited fewer serotonin receptors than those who never express such yearnings.

Before drawing too close of a correlation between religiosity and the number of type-1A serotonin receptors, we should recognize that other features of the brain also correlate with the tendency to rate one's self as religious. A recent investigation discovered that the tendency to display extravagant religious behaviors correlated significantly with atrophy (i.e., shrinkage) of the right hippocampus in patients with untreatable epilepsy.

In fact, the medical literature is replete with reports of epilepsy patients with religious delusions. Decreased brain activity in the hippocampus has also been correlated with the feeling of a "sensed presence" or the eerie feeling of an unseen person nearby. Recent studies using sophisticated brain imaging techniques also suggest that the prefrontal cortex is more likely involved in controlling our religious, moral, and paranormal beliefs.

To understand why the brain generates religious sensations under these unusual conditions, it is necessary to appreciate what it does under normal circumstances. Usually, your brain receives sensory inputs from your body and produces a sense of where you are in the world, what you are doing at this moment, and what is happening all around you. This incoming information is constantly updated and provides you with a sense of "self." If your senses are impaired or your brain's ability to interpret sensory information is altered because of an hallucinogenic drug or a disorder like epilepsy, your brain is forced to do the best it can with what it has working; thus, under these conditions, you might have some very unusual sensory experiences, such as feelings of floating in space, a connection to everything in the universe, or a communication with your god, however you might see him or her.

You can clearly see that, for lack of any more precise way to quantify these experiences, neuroscientists often describe religious phenomena in terms of neurobiological processes whose activity or inactivity they can observe with their brain scanners. Indeed, there might not be anything more to a religious experience than the activation of the right dorsal region of the hippocampus, or the inactivation of the top part of our parietal lobe (to name but two currently appealing hypotheses). On the other hand, perhaps these changes in brain activity that neuroscientists are observing with their modern scanners are simply the brain's response to an actual communication from God! After all, how else would your creator be able to communicate with you except by way of the sensory systems that your brain uses to experience reality?

SUMMARY

Serotonin neurons project diffusely and broadly throughout the entire brain, and so their effects are difficult to summarize. One important clue to the function of this neurotransmitter system is that its neurons seem to dribble serotonin from their projections constantly and uniformly throughout our waking periods and to slow down dramatically when we are asleep. From this we can hypothesize that serotonin is involved with processing the incoming sensory information that constantly bombards our brain while we are awake. How this happens is not yet known with certainty. However, when we ingest drugs that turn off our serotonin neurons while we are awake, we experience sensory hallucinations characterized by synesthesia, or the mixing of sensory modalities, and often by a mystical sense of higher consciousness. By contrast, our most effective antidepressants enhance the function of serotonin in the brain. The fact that these drugs are so effective does not prove that mood regulation

is the normal role of serotonin in the brain but may rather demonstrate that how we interpret sensory information is related to
how we feel about the world around us.

Serotonin is not the only neurotransmitter whose manipulation can produce hallucinations. In fact, the neurotransmitter
system introduced in Chapter 5 can be altered to cause similar
hallucinatory effects and, for that matter, to bring about a host
of experiences (e.g., euphoria) similar to those that occur with
the manipulation of other neurotransmitters.

MARIJUANA IN THE BRAIN

What drug is enjoyable and, under some circumstances, might actually be good for your brain? Can smoking this substance prevent age-related memory loss, for example? To answer these and similar questions, I turn now to a neurotransmitter system in the brain that was discovered through the use of one of the most common drugs in our history. This system may not have the most familiar of names—endogenous cannabinoid neurotransmitter—but the drug that tells us most about its function is certainly a household word: marijuana. Indeed, few drugs have the kind of colorful history that marijuana has achieved. Thus, before examining the neurotransmitter that it affects, let's look briefly at the story of the drug itself.

DOPE AND A ROPE

Among species of marijuana plants, *Cannabis indica* is the one grown principally for its psychoactive resins. It is likely a shorter, bushier version of the *Cannabis sativa*, which is used primarily for its fibers to make rope. Both plants, like catnip, contain active ingredients belonging to a family of compounds called terpenes, of which the primary psychoactive terpene is thought to be concentrated in the plants' resin as delta-9 tetrahydrocannabinol (THC). Initially investigated more than 100 years ago by two chemists, the Smith Brothers (William and Andrew) of later cough-drop fame, the plants contain approximately 50 cannabinoid-based compounds, with 4 major cannabinoids: trans-delta-9-THC and delta-8-THC, cannabidiol (the second most abundant psychoactive ingredient after THC), and cannabinol, which may be a decomposition product of THC that accumulates as cannabis samples age. After ingestion, the trans-delta-9-THC is converted in the liver to 11-hydroxy THC, which is equally potent and psychoactive.

Probably the oldest reference to the cannabis plant, in a pharmacy book from 2737 BCE, is related to its use as a medicine. The Chinese emperor Shen Nung (*the Divine Farmer*) referred to it as the "liberator of sin" and recommended it for the treatment of "female weakness," gout, rheumatism, malaria, constipation, and absent mindedness. By 1000 BCE, its medicinal use, as indicated by available writings, had spread to India; by 500 BCE, it was familiar to the ancient Greeks.

The earliest reference to the use of cannabis as an inebriant was in 430 BCE, when the Greek historian Herodotus of Halicarnassus wrote that the Scythians burned the seeds and inhaled the smoke to induce intoxication during funerals. The plant is also mentioned several times (as "kaneh-bosem," קְנֵה-בֹשֶׂם) in the Old Testament (as Yahweh's instruction to Moses in Exodus 30:23) as a bartering material, incense, and an ingredient in holy anointing oil; it was likely used by the high priests of the temple as well as by Jesus. At that time in history, the word messiah simply meant "the anointed one." Use of the plant as an inebriant spread to the Muslim world and North Africa by 1000 CE and became epidemic by the 12th century. The exploring Spaniards likely brought *kaneh-bos*, by now probably pronounced as *cannabis*, to the New World in about 1545.

Meanwhile, let's not forget that other, more humdrum role that cannabis has played in history. English settlers brought it, as well as tobacco, to Jamestown, Virginia by 1611 and used its fibers to make rope. In the 1700s, George Washington grew cannabis on his farm and, according to entries in his diary, maintained a keen interest in cultivating better strains of the plant, evidently for the purpose of producing a better quality of rope. In 1942, the U.S. government made a number of movie-shorts aimed at encouraging farmers to plant hemp, or cannabis, for wartime use as rope. Other rather famous historical uses of cannabis fiber are said to include Chinese paper, the ropes and sails on Christopher Columbus's ships, the Declaration of

Independence, World War II parachutes, and the first Levi jeans.

Today, when most people hear the term *marijuana*, they think of the leafy material from *C. indica* that is generally smoked. It contains 2% to 5% THC. Sinsemilla or ganja, made from the unpollinated female cannabis plant, may contain up to 15% THC. Hashish, which is actually the Arabic word for grass (which might explain the slang term for this plant), is made from a dried concentrate of the resin of cannabis flowers and contains about 8% to 14% THC. Hashish oil typically has from 15% to 60% THC, and bhang, a drink popular in India that is made of cannabis leaves, milk, sugar, and spices, has 2% to 5% THC. Kief (from the Arabic *kaif* كيف meaning "pleasure, well being") is made from the dried resin of *C. indica* and usually has very high THC levels. Budder is a processed and concentrated form of hashish oil that is reported to contain between 82% to 99% THC by weight. Given its potency and effectiveness, it probably takes a lot of bread to buy this budder.

Whatever its form, marijuana is today categorized as a gateway drug for its role in leading users to try other illegal drugs. Overall, statistics show that very few young people use other illegal drugs without first trying marijuana. However, the majority of marijuana users (about 60%) do not go on to use any other illicit drugs. By contrast, according to some statistics, most users report having tried legal substances—cigarettes or beer—before trying marijuana. Thus, tobacco and alcohol products could be considered gateway drugs as well. It's worth pointing out that that alcohol is considered as addictive as heroin, and tobacco is considered as addictive as crack cocaine.

What does marijuana do in the brain? It produces some excitatory behavioral changes, including euphoria, but it is not generally regarded as a stimulant. It can also produce some sedative effects but not to the extent of a barbiturate or alcohol. It produces mild analgesic effects (pain relief) as well, but this action is not related pharmacologically to the pain-relieving effects of opiates or aspirin (*see* Chapter 8). Finally, marijuana produces hallucinations at high doses, but its structure does not resemble LSD or any other drug formally categorized as a hallucinogen. Thus, marijuana's effects on our body and brain are complex. Just how does it achieve these effects?

THE BRAIN'S OWN MARIJUANA-LIKE NEUROTRANSMITTER

The very high potency and structure of the cannabinoids contained within the marijuana plant enable them to cross the blood–brain barrier and bind to a receptor for the brain's very own endogenous cannabinoid neurotransmitter system. If this were not true, then the marijuana plant would be popular only for its use in making rope, paper, and cloth. The two currently identified neurotransmitters compounds (and there are probably more) in this system are anandamide, from the Sanskrit word *ananda* (आनन्द) meaning "bliss," and 2-AG (2-arachidonoyl-glycerol). Unlike the other neurotransmitters that I've discussed, these two "endocannabinoids" are not stored in synaptic vesicles.

Rather, they are both produced within neurons and released to flow backward across the synapse to find their receptors, designated as CB1 and CB2. There are probably more of these CB receptors for marijuana in the human brain than for any other known neurotransmitter. The great abundance of these receptors and their widespread location gives an indication of importance of the endocannabinoid system in the regulation of the brain's normal functioning.

Let's take a look at what these endocannabinoids do in the brain to gain some insight into the consequences of smoking (or eating) marijuana. For example, anandamide inhibits the release of glutamate and acetylcholine within the cortex and hippocampus, an action that may underlie the ability of marijuana to impair one's capacity to form new memories when using the drug. The presence of cannabinoid receptors in the parts of the brain that control movement may underlie the stumbling behavior that some marijuana users experience. Cannabinoid receptors greatly enhance the release of dopamine; this action plays a critical role in the ability of marijuana to produce euphoria. Finally, stimulation of cannabinoid receptors in the feeding centers of the hypothalamus may underlie the classic marijuana side effect known as the "munchies."

This last effect coincidentally drew the attention of scientists who conducted a series of clinical trials using a drug that blocks the brain's cannabinoid receptors. Their hope was that this drug's blocking action would produce an "anti-munchies" effect, thereby reducing food consumption and providing help to overweight patients. At first, the drug worked fairly well. People reported being less attracted to eating. Unfortunately, they also became severely depressed. What this discovery tells scientists is that our endogenous cannabinoid system is normally involved, either directly or indirectly, in elevating or controlling our mood and that antagonizing the cannabinoid receptors in the brain, as occurred with this novel drug, can produce some dangerous consequences.

In contrast, stimulating the brain's cannabinoid receptors may offer protection from the consequences of stroke, chronic pain, and neuro-inflammation. Surprisingly, it may also protect against some aspects of age-associated memory loss. Ordinarily, we do not view marijuana as being good for our brain and certainly not for making memories. How could a drug that clearly impairs memory while people are under its sway protect their brains from the consequences of aging?

The answer likely has everything to do with the way that young and old brains function and the age-related changes in the actions of the neurotransmitters acetylcholine and glutamate. These two neurotransmitters are involved in making new memories and destroying old or unnecessary ones. Early in life, this process of creation and destruction is in balance, and so interfering with it—such as occurs when using marijuana—might impair memory. But later in life, the roles of these neurotransmitters change in significant ways. In addition, the aged brain displays increasing evidence of inflammation and a dramatic decline in the production of new neurons, called neurogenesis.

Marijuana may offer protection in at least three different ways: by preventing the damaging actions of glutamate, by reducing brain inflammation, and by restoring neurogenesis. Thus, later in life, marijuana might actually help your brain, rather than harm it. Research in my laboratory by Dr. Yannick Marchalant suggests that it takes very little marijuana to produce benefits in the older brain; his motto is "a puff is enough." The challenge for pharmacologists in the future will be to isolate the beneficial aspects of cannabinoid manipulation from its psychoactive effects, which themselves can be an additional burden to those suffering from the consequences of these conditions.

SUMMARY

Once again, the distribution of a neurotransmitter provides clues to its function in the brain. For example, our brains' endogenous cannabinoid neurons are in the hypothalamus feeding centers; when these receptors are stimulated, we feel hungry, and when they are blocked, we become less interested in eating. Cannabinoid neurons also influence the function of our cortex and various limbic (emotion-controlling) regions; when we stimulate these receptors, we impair higher cognitive functions as we experience euphoria, and when they are blocked, we feel depression. Because our brain appears to have a large number of different types of neurons that are affected by marijuana, a complete explanation of this drug's effects remains nearly impossible. What seems clear, however, is that the endogenous cannabinoid neurotransmitters that our brain produces do not appear to transmit information *per se* but appear to modulate how other neurotransmitter systems function. In this way, they act quite differently from the manner in which the neurotransmitters discussed in Chapter 6 behave.

SIMPLE MOLECULES THAT TURN YOU ON AND OFF

W hy is a drug like PCP potentially lethal? Why does drinking alcohol make you drowsy? How do anti-anxiety drugs work, and why is it so dangerous to take them and alcohol at the same time? The answers to these questions have everything to do with the most abundant neurotransmitters in your brain, simple amino acids that are used for two simple functions: to turn on or off individual neurons. When used for communication, neurons usually respond to amino acid neurotransmitters—principally glutamate and GABA—with either excitation or inhibition. Glutamate is the principal excitatory amino acid neurotransmitter, whereas GABA is the principal inhibitory amino acid neurotransmitter.

GLUTAMATE

What is so important about glutamate? It makes and breaks connections between neurons, and it turns on other neurons to stimulate them into action. Glutamate neurotransmission is mediated through receptors that allow the passage of sodium or calcium ions into neurons; the receptors were named according to the chemical tools that were historically used to study them. For example, the subtype of glutamate receptors known as N-methyl-D-Aspartate (NMDA) allows the entry of calcium ions into neurons. Following the entry of calcium ions, some truly interesting things begin to happen inside the neuron that leads to the production of what you might call a "memory." Calcium ions activate a complex cascade of biochemical changes that ultimately involve the genes of the neuron and that may actually change how the neuron behaves for the rest of your life. These biochemical changes may also alter how one neuron communicates with hundreds of other neurons.

Think of this neural process as a symphony of musicians playing together for the first time. Initially, everyone is playing his or her own song. Then the conductor arrives and hands out a musical score; all of the musicians begin to play in a complex pattern of rhythms that conveys information. Like the conductor, calcium ions entering via NMDA channels initiate the process of forming an ensemble of neuronal activity. Your neurons are the musicians, and when they become linked to each other according to some common pattern of activity, they form an ensemble that plays a particular song, or memory, which can recur only when that particular ensemble of neurons plays the same pattern together. In this analogy, memories can be seen as symphonies of activity in our brains, and just as we enjoy playing the same tunes over and over again, so we also enjoy replaying pleasant memories. Unfortunately, glutamate's actions can prime us to play unpleasant or traumatic memories over and over again as well when they are triggered by innocent events in our daily lives.

In addition, the entry of calcium ions into neurons may sometimes become excessive as a result of aging, disease, or stroke and may initiate some harmful processes that may contribute to the removal of synapses or even the death of neurons. This information tells us quite a lot about the role of glutamate: when it works correctly, memories can be formed; when it does not work correctly, as when it induces too much calcium to enter the neuron, then death and destruction follow and memory is lost. Thus, maintaining a good balance of function related to the entry of calcium ions is a challenging but critical requirement for neurons, and the amino acid neurotransmitter glutamate plays a critical role in this process.

Glutamate also has a unique function in brain development. When you were very young, the neurons in your brain developed many connections, or synapses, with other neurons to optimize your ability to learn a great deal of information quickly, such as how to move your hands and feet, what your mother's voice sounds like, or what the color red looks like. But as you grew older (during adolescence), your brain became a bit like an over-wired computer—for it to work better and faster, with less likelihood of failing, it became advantageous for it to remove unnecessary "wires," or connections. This is where glutamate's other unique abilities come into play. Your brain uses glutamate to prune synapses that have become unnecessary, which in turn allows the remaining neural circuits to function more efficiently. Later, when you're an adult, glutamate is critical for allowing your brain to be "plastic," to mold your responses to the environment so that you increase your chances of survival. Thus, like the Roman god Janus, the neurotransmitter glutamate has two faces: One is important for the early brain development and function in our past; the other is important for brain pruning and subsequent function in our future. Meanwhile, its staying power can sometimes be a mixed blessing. For example, as mentioned, traumatic memories formed through glutamate's actions can continue to haunt us long after the event that created those memories has occurred. The best example of this is called post-traumatic stress disorder; the unpleasant memories that characterize this disorder are very difficult to treat because of the amazing efficacy of glutamate to form lasting changes in the brain.

Currently, very few safe drugs are used clinically to target glutamate receptors. But there are two drugs of abuse, phencyclidine (aka PCP or Angel Dust) and ketamine, which can antagonize the NMDA type of glutamate receptor. Because these drugs block this principal excitatory neurotransmitter, they depress your brain's general level of activity. Your brain's information processing simply slows further and further until it can no longer keep you conscious. Phencyclidine was once used as an anesthetic with some unfortunate consequences. Patients lost the ability to breathe, they became delirious and disoriented, and their heart rate decreased so much that they sometimes slipped into a coma and died.

Because phencyclidine is so potent, scientists believe that the brain makes its own endogenous PCP-like molecule, now named angeldustin should it one day be isolated. Recent studies have suggested that reduced function of angeldustin may actually contribute to certain psychiatric syndromes, such as mania, and cause too much activity of the glutamate receptors in the brains of manic patients. Others have suggested that whatever the cause, increased function of the brain's principal excitatory neurotransmitter drives the symptoms of mania such as racing thoughts, insomnia, and impulsiveness. That said, the medical treatment of mania, usually with the use of a salt called lithium chloride, does not involve reducing glutamate neuronal function but instead slows the manic brain by very different mechanisms. One of these mechanisms may be related to lithium's ability to induce the birth of new GABA-releasing neurons, of which the brains of manic patients have a reduced number. This possibility would make sense given the particular nature of that neurotransmitter. In any case, too much inhibition of glutamate would severely impair the brain's ability to process information. Our brains need to have glutamate's excitatory actions working appropriately for us to learn and pay attention. Rather than reduce an overactive brain by using drugs that inhibit glutamate, humans have discovered many different drugs that force our brains to slow down by stimulating the function of GABA neurons.

γ-AMINOBUTYRIC ACID

In contrast to glutamate, the amino acid neurotransmitter GABA turns neurons off. After being released into the synaptic space, it binds to a protein receptor. The best studied of these is the $GABA_A$ receptor, and drugs that bind to it enhance the ability of GABA to stabilize the activity of the neuron. In so doing, these drugs have produced dramatic therapeutic benefits for a wide range of disorders, particularly for the treatment of anxiety and insomnia. Why should this be the case? There are two simple reasons: GABA receptors are widely distributed throughout all brain regions, and GABA is virtually always inhibitory. Thus, any drug that enhances GABA receptor function produces an overall decrease in the activity of neurons *everywhere* in your brain. You cannot, contrary to the claims made in popular magazines, accomplish this effect simply by eating GABA-containing substances to increase the amount of GABA in your brain. While floating in the bloodstream, ingested GABA becomes electrically charged, preventing it from passing across the blood–brain barrier. Taking a few hundred milligrams of GABA everyday, therefore, will not reduce your anxiety or help you sleep. Instead, your treatments of choice are drugs that turn on your existing GABA receptors to turn off your brain, either a little to reduce your anxiety or a lot to make you sleep. Although recent evidence suggests that anxiety, like depression and migraine headaches, may be related to serotonin receptor dysfunction more than to GABA, medical science prefers to treat anxiety with prescription, GABA-enhancing drugs, which do work to reduce this symptom. What do the actions of these drugs tell us about the causes of anxiety in the brain? Not that much. Again, simply because it is possible to treat the symptoms of a disorder by manipulating a particular neurotransmitter system in the brain does not tell us anything about the actual cause of the disorder. All we can say with certainty is that if you're feeling anxious, taking one of these drugs will make you feel less so.

SPECIFIC DRUGS THAT ENHANCE THE ACTION OF GABA IN THE BRAIN

Among the earliest anti-anxiety drugs were the sleep-inducing hypnotics, which essentially depress activity in the brain and make it difficult to feel anything at all. Various salts of the halide bromine were used to reduce brain activity associated with epilepsy, anxiety, or stress. Fans of old movies set in a bygone era may remember the occasional actress holding her forehead and stating that she needed to "take a Bromo" to treat a headache. Although these salts were effective at reducing the neural activity in the brain that is required to experience pain, or to even maintain wakefulness, they were extremely toxic to the kidneys and ultimately removed from the commercial market. They were replaced by opiates, which were available without restriction during the 18th and 19th centuries. So was a more popular and socially acceptable drug that in many cultures, including our own, still has almost iconic status today.

Alcohol

Alcohol (ethyl, not methyl) may have been the first anxiety-reducing agent. There is evidence that distillation of grains to make alcohol-containing beverages, what today we would refer to as beer, may have begun in the "Fertile Cresent" (between present day Iran, Iraq, Syria, and Israel) by about 10000 BCE. The ancient Egyptians also produced alcoholic beverages, referring in some passages within their texts to the social problems associated with drunkenness. Other Egyptian texts, written around 1600 BCE, contained 100 different medical prescriptions calling for the use of alcohol. Over subsequent centuries, several types of alcohol, distilled and fermented, were developed, and they all had their calming effects. In fact, because alcohol enhances the action of the neurotransmitter GABA, it can depress the activity of the entire brain. For this reason, in the 19th century, alcohol was widely used as a general anesthetic. Unfortunately, the duration of its depressant action on the brain was too long and could not be controlled easily or safely. The effective dose for surgical analgesia using alcohol is very close to its lethal dose. Thus, if you lived in the 19th century and were shot in the leg, you could be sufficiently anesthetized with alcohol so as to have the bullet surgically removed, but it would be unlikely that you'd survive the operation.

In addition to its actions upon GABA receptors, alcohol inhibits the brain's principal excitatory neurotransmitter system, glutamate. Given glutamate's critical role in making memories, this inhibitory effect may underlie the amnesia that is often associated with intoxication—that is, the classic blackout. It may also explain the inappropriate behavior that often occurs when people drink. My students complain about this behavior among their friends following consumption of only modest amounts of alcohol. The apparent stimulation of the brain after a small dose of alcohol may result in unrestrained activity of various brain regions caused by the lessening of their inhibitory controls. Which specific behaviors are released and which are depressed depends on the person and his or her history of drug usage. Usually, alcohol consumption releases punished behaviors (e.g., behavior that was suppressed by an aversive stimulus such as the memory of your mother warning you not to dance naked in the park at midnight).

As with most drugs that affect your brain, the rate at which your blood alcohol levels rise also affect your behavior—that is, faster changes in blood alcohol levels produce more dramatic effects on your behavior. As alcohol levels increase, more and more of your brain is turned off by alcohol's enhancement of GABA. Ultimately, when blood levels become too high, neurons critical to controlling your breathing and heart rate are inactivated because of overstimulation of their GABA receptors. Therefore, death resulting from alcohol intoxication occurs because you stop breathing. Usually, before that happens, your brain's vomiting control center will become activated at blood alcohol levels of about 0.12%. However, if you drink slowly and steadily, you can sneak up on these protective neurons and inactivate them with alcohol. Once this happens, your body makes no effort to rid itself of alcohol in the stomach by vomiting and the levels of alcohol in your blood can continue to rise to lethal levels. Thus, vomiting at the end of the party is a good thing, really. Your body is trying to protect you.

Barbiturates

At the end of the 19th century, it was obvious that an alternative drug for anxiety was necessary that would be safer than the popular and highly available alcohol and opium. In 1904, the first barbiturate barbital was introduced and sold as Veronal. It was a nontoxic sedative, and because of its anticonvulsant properties, it also appeared to be ideal for treating and preventing the symptoms of epilepsy. As you might have guessed already, barbiturates reduce neural activity in the brain by enhancing the function of GABA receptors and producing widespread synaptic inhibition, just like alcohol.

Just how safe the barbiturates are is subject to much debate. For one thing, in high doses, they are lethal, the reason that for many years barbiturate overdose was a common way by which people committed suicide. In addition, the rebound produced by withdrawal from barbiturates is characterized by increased neural activity throughout the brain, leading to symptoms that are often the motivation for taking these drugs in the first place, such as anxiety, disorientation, hallucinations, convulsions, insomnia, tachycardia, or nightmares. The fact that alcohol can prevent the withdrawal symptoms of barbiturates shows the commonality of their action at the GABA receptor. This commonality underlies the reason that alcohol and barbiturates produce a synergistic toxicity in the brain. What this means is that these drugs should never be taken together because their effects will be compounded, or even multiplied, and can induce a dramatic and possibly permanent loss of higher brain function, leading to a vegetative state or coma. This array of potentially life-threatening risks associated with barbiturates led to the introduction of an entirely new class of anti-anxiety medications to the market.

Benzodiazepines

The first benzodiazepine, chlordiazepoxide, was initially synthesized in 1947 and first sold commercially in 1960 as Librium (because it produced an emotional equilibrium). Shortly thereafter, diazepam was sold as Valium (Latin for "be strong and well") and quickly became the most prescribed anti-anxiety drug in the western world. Both of these drugs are converted into other psychoactive agents within the brain and body. Some of these metabolites were isolated from the urine of people taking Valium and Librium and were discovered to be quite effective new drugs that could reduce anxiety and produce sleepiness. Because of changes in lipid solubility, these newer drugs acted upon the brain faster and, as typically follows, had a shorter duration of action. They are generally safe to use in controlled doses, but once again, withdrawal from them produces abrupt increases in widespread neural activity that is often expressed as insomnia and anxiety. Recently, an even newer class of drugs called nonbenzodiazepines was introduced to consumers, and these drugs also reduce anxiety and induce sleepiness.

All of these drugs, benzodiazepine and non-benzodiazepine alike, exert their effects only in presence of GABA, enhancing the action of GABA at its receptor. The highest concentration of these receptors is found in the neocortex, hippocampus, cerebellum, and throughout the limbic system (which is involved in producing both pleasant and unpleasant emotional responses). The presence of these receptors within the hippocampus may explain why benzodiazepines can produce amnesia. They may inactivate the neural circuits in this structure that are critical for the consolidation of memories.

Recent studies suggest that the brain may contain its own family of valium-like compounds, the β-carbolines. Some of these antagonize GABA function and others enhance it, but all may share a similar ability to inhibit the destruction of the neurotransmitters dopamine, norepinephrine, and serotonin; taken together, these effects would tend to produce a mild, relaxed euphoria. The balance of action of these endogenous anti-anxiety compounds is determined by the genes we inherit from our parents, which control the carbolines produced and probably predispose us to being anxious or laidback throughout our lives. It is now thought that anxiety disorders may be related to a dysfunction of GABA receptors and the balance of function of these carbolines.

Indeed, scientists have speculated that the brains of people who suffer from generalized anxiety disorder may produce too many of these chemicals from their diet. True, some carbolines can be formed spontaneously from the constituents of our diet. For example, coffee produces β-carbolines, and alcohol can be converted by bacterium in the gut, *Helicobacter pylori*, to form a β-carboline. Whether these exogenous β-carbolines are produced in sufficient quantities to produce functional consequences in the brain remains to be determined. We do know, however, that the carbolines in the brain are similar to those found, for example, in the *Banisteriopsis caapi* vine; extracts of the vine are a key ingredient in the mildly psychoactive sacramental beverage *Ayahuasca* from the Amazon. Because the ingredients in these vines, known as harmala alkaloids, resemble molecules used by your brain, their consumption can influence how you think and feel. It perhaps stands to reason then, if not yet confirmed in fact, that consuming exogenous β-carbolines to correct an endogenous imbalance of these molecules would have a similar influence on the brain.

Absinthe and a GABA Antagonist

What would it feel like if you ingested a drug that blocked the brain's most important inhibitory neurotransmitter? Would you become excited? Thujone is such a drug; it blocks the action of

GABA at one of its principal receptors in the brain. Thujone can be found in many different plants, but it is most often associated with wormwood (*Artemisia absinthium*), the extract of which, when mixed with alcohol, produces a bright green drink called absinthe. During the mid-1800s, this drink became very popular in Europe, especially among such artists as Manet, Degas, Toulouse-Lautrec, and Van Gogh. The ritual was to pour the emerald-green liquid slowly over sugar held in a perforated spoon and then diluted with water. The taste was very bitter, and the drink was said to produce a "lucid drunkenness." Then, during the late 1800s, studies by the French psychiatrist Valentin Magnan discovered that wormwood oil produced inappropriately increased brain activity—in short, an epileptic reaction. Thus, it was thought that the effects of chronic use of absinthe, such as contractions of the face muscles and extremities, anxiety, paranoia, energy loss, numbness, headaches, delirium, paralysis, and death, resulted from the existence of thujone in the wormwood extract used in this drink. The *American Journal of Pharmacy* wrote in 1868 that "it's an ignoble poison, destroying life not until it has more or less brutalized its votaries, and made driveling idiots of them." A campaign against thujone ensued and resulted, by the early 20th century, in the banning of absinthe in many countries, including in the United States.

Today, however, it is known that the manner in which absinthe was once prepared would have produced only very low levels of thujone in a typical serving. Therefore, the symptoms noted among chronic users of absinthe more likely resulted from the excessive consumption of improperly distilled spirits rather than to the effects of thujone. To be sure, thujone is a GABA antagonist and can produce excitatory effects in small doses, but these effects are mild. It can be found in very low amounts in drinks such as vermouth (from the German *wermuth* for wormwood), chartreuse, and Benedictine. Of course, it remains in similarly small amounts in absinthe, the legal sale of which has now resumed in most countries.

SUMMARY

When you think of glutamate, you should imagine the words *on, excitation,* and *plasticity.* Our brains are very plastic thanks to this neurotransmitter system. The actions of glutamate shape our brains in so many important ways. Glutamate prunes synaptic connections between neurons when they are not needed, makes new ones when they are, stimulates neurons to become excited and process new information, and destroys neurons when they are not working correctly or are no longer needed. As we age, this process of destruction can sometimes go too far and produce impairments in the function of our brains. Drugs that block the action of glutamate usually interfere with plasticity and impair brain function. However, these drugs may one day find use in the prevention of Alzheimer's and Parkinson's diseases.

In contrast, when you think about GABA, you should imagine the word *off.* Whenever drugs enhance the function of GABA in the brain, usually lots and lots of neurons are being turned off. Most of the drugs discussed in this chapter act by enhancing the actions of GABA, leading to reduced brain activity that sometimes, such as when alcohol and barbiturates are combined, can be lethal. Suffice it to say that GABA neurons are distributed throughout the brain; therefore, it is possible to turn off the entire brain by taking too many drugs that enhance GABA simultaneously. Essentially, as the activity of ever more neurons is slowed, we gradually fall asleep; then, with ever more inhibition of brain function, we can even die: The Big Sleep.

CHAPTER 7

Sleeping Versus Waking

Why do treatments for the symptoms of the common cold make us drowsy? How does coffee work? This chapter touches briefly on neurotransmitters whose actions in the brain affect our sleep–wake cycle and on a few well-known substances that block these effects.

HISTAMINE AND OREXIN

One such neurotransmitter is histamine, whose neurons influence our level of arousal throughout the day. Lying next to these neurons is another group of neurons that release orexin, which is a neurotransmitter that influences both our level of arousal and craving for food. Take a moment to appreciate how the anatomical organization of this system optimizes your daily existence and survival. The neurons that wake you in the morning and maintain your consciousness also make you crave food. In contrast, the inactivation of these two brain regions makes you sleepy and reduces the activity of your food-craving center in the brain. The failure of the orexin arousal-inducing system may underlie narcolepsy, a disorder characterized by inappropriate and intense sleepiness.

Over-the-counter anti-histamine medications used to treat allergies and cold symptoms block histamine receptors and interfere with the ability of this neurotransmitter to keep one aroused and awake. The result is drowsiness. Meanwhile, because GABA neurons induce sleepiness by turning off histamine and acetylcholine neurons, any drug that enhances the action of GABA (e.g., alcohol, barbiturates, or Valium) is going to be synergistic with the over-the-counter anti-histamine drugs. Thus, if taken together, these two kinds of drugs can bring about a life-threatening depression in brain activity.

ADENOSINE

This neurotransmitter has diverse functions throughout the brain that are also related to our sleep–wake cycles. We know a lot about it because of the ready availability of a very safe, highly effective adenosine receptor antagonist that is served hot or cold, with or without cream, throughout the world—caffeinated coffee! Caffeine is also commonly found with theophylline (a molecule that is very similar to caffeine) in tea. Indeed, although caffeine is found in at least 63 plant species, 54% of the world's consumption derives from just two different beans, *Coffea arabica* and *Coffea robusta*, and 43% derives from the tea plant *Camellia sinensis*.

Coffee is rich in biologically active substances such as trigonelline, quinolinic acid, tannic acid, and pyrogallic acid. The vitamin niacin is formed in great amounts from trigonelline during the coffee bean roasting process. Coffee is also a rich source of the antioxidants caffeic, chlorogenic, coumaric, ferrulic, and sinapic acids and silverskin. Various ingredients in coffee beans contribute to aspects of the drink—for example, its bitterness—that people find either appealing or unpleasant. Recently, some entrepreneurs have found a way to remove the bitterness by "filtering" coffee beans through the gastrointestinal tract of the Asian Palm Civet, *Paradoxurus hermaphroditus*. The civets, nocturnal omnivores that are about the size of a cat, eat the beans, which then pass through the animals' gastrointestinal systems undigested but presumably not unaffected. The beans are then extracted from the animals' stool, cleaned up, and sold. It's hardly an enticing process, but the claim is that the animal's digestive enzymes metabolize the proteins that cause the bitter taste of the coffee bean. Although this is certainly possible, the novel flavor of the beans is just as likely a result of the bean's absorption of some of the less appealing contents of the animals' gut.

Coffee drinking (or consuming caffeine from non-coffee sources) has been associated with a significantly lowered risk of developing Parkinson's disease. The neuroprotective effect requires about five to six cups of coffee per day for many years and appears to be mostly beneficial only to males. Women benefit from coffee-drinking in other ways, particularly with regard to a reduced incidence of type-2 diabetes. Overall, people who drink substantial amounts of coffee daily tend to live longer than people who do not. In addition, recent evidence suggests that moderate coffee-drinking of about two to three cups each day might reduce your chance of developing Alzheimer's disease. What is the connection among coffee, diabetes, and diseases of the brain? No one is sure, but elevated insulin levels in the blood may be a critical link because type-2 diabetes makes both men and women more likely to develop both Parkinson's and Alzheimer's disease.

Many people drink coffee to reduce drowsiness. How does caffeine achieve this effect in the brain? The answer begins with a consideration of the function of the acetylcholine neurons that control your ability to pay attention. Adenosine negatively controls the activity of these neurons, meaning that when adenosine binds to its receptor on acetylcholine neurons, their activity slows. The production and release of adenosine in your brain is linked to metabolic activity while you are awake. Therefore, the concentration of adenosine in the neighborhood of acetylcholine neurons increases constantly while your brain is active during the day. As the levels of adenosine increase, they steadily inhibit your acetylcholine neurons, your brain's activity gradually slows, and you begin to feel drowsy and ultimately fall asleep. Caffeine comes to the rescue because it, like theophylline from tea, is a potent blocker of adenosine receptors and, therefore, of the adenosine-driven drowsiness and sleep. One can take this too far, however. One of my students decided to test these caffeine effects by ingesting a packet of instant coffee, right out of the box. He reported that he enjoyed eating it so much that he decided to finish off the entire container of 32 packets! Three days later, he stopped having explosive diarrhea and finally fell asleep completely exhausted.

Given everything that you've read about drugs that produce a rewarding and euphoric feeling, you might suspect that coffee also somehow affects dopamine neurons. You would be correct. Caffeine sets free the activity of dopamine neurons to bring euphoria and bliss to every cup of coffee or every glass of cola. Most cans of cola contain about 40 milligrams of caffeine; therefore, most teenagers consume as much caffeine as their parents—the only thing that differs is the vehicle for the drug. The widespread availability of foods containing caffeine has led experts to suggest that 80% of all people in North America have measureable levels of caffeine in their brains from embryo to death.

Caffeine and theophylline are not the only drugs we regularly consume to block our adenosine receptors. There is also theobromine, which is found in chocolate. Chocolate is as addicting as coffee—if not more so—possibly because it contains an array of other psychoactive compounds that may contribute to the pleasurable sensation of eating it. Chocolate contains fats that may induce the release of endogenous opiates (*see* Chapter 8) and produce a feeling of euphoria. It contains phenethylamine, a molecule that resembles amphetamine and some of the other psychoactive stimulants discussed earlier. It contains a small amount of the marijuana-like neurotransmitter anandamide. It contains some estrogen-like compounds, a fact that may explain a recent series of reports showing that men who eat chocolate live longer than men who do not eat chocolate (the effect was not seen for women who have an ample supply of their own estrogen until menopause). Chocolate also contains magnesium salts, the absence of which in elderly females may be responsible for the common post-menopausal condition known as chocoholism. And finally, a standard bar of chocolate contains as many anti-oxidants as a glass of red wine. Clearly, there are many good reasons for men and women to eat chocolate to obtain its indescribably soothing, mellow, and yet euphoric effect, with or without the addition of caffeine. My fear, of course, is that one day the Food and Drug Administration may take notice of the many psychoactive compounds present in chocolate and regulate its sale.

SUMMARY

Histamine-releasing neuronal projects arise from the bottom of our brains and play a role in arousing us. Blocking the function of histamine with cold medications makes us drowsy and makes performing complex tasks difficult, such as operating heavy machinery or driving, which we are all warned not to do while taking these drugs!

Adenosine is ubiquitous in the brain. Every cell can release it and does so rather continually while you are awake. It builds in concentration and slowly inhibits the activity of nearby neurons. Of particular concern is the inhibition of the attention-controlling acetylcholine neurons that project to the cortex. We need and want those neurons to be active so we consume drinks containing caffeine, a drug that quickly enters the brain and blocks the action of adenosine and releases acetylcholine neurons from the tyranny of inactivation: once again, coffee comes to the rescue.

CHAPTER 8

Remnants of an Ancient Past

Very primitive multicellular organisms, such as the hydra (e.g., *Chlorohydra viridissima*, the ultimate simple feeding tube), have nervous systems that may only use simple proteins as neurotransmitters, suggesting that these proteins were the first signaling molecules used by primordial nervous systems. If we extract a few of these proteins from the "brain" of a typical Hydra and inject them in human neurons, they will actually produce similar signaling responses from those neurons.

In fact, the proteins used by hydra in their nervous systems are identical to some of the proteins that our brains use to help us think and feel. These proteins are called neuropeptides. A neuropeptide is like a string of beads, and each bead is an amino acid. Neuropeptides may be assembled from only a few or from hundreds of different amino acids. Your body contains many different types of neuropeptides that are assembled from the amino acids found in your diet. Neurons that produce and release these neuropeptides are found throughout the body and brain and influence a diverse array of body functions, including the release of hormones and the absorption of nutrients from our blood.

The evolutionary history of our neuropeptides is quite interesting and tells us a great deal about their current role and why they are found in certain places in the body and not others. One very important neuropeptide is insulin, which is produced by the pancreas. Some neuroscientists have speculated that an insulin-like peptide might have been the principal ancestor to many of our other neuropeptides that are still structurally related to each other. For example, growth hormone and prolactin, peptides that control breast development and milk production, respectively, may have diverged from a common ancestor about 350 million years ago. Therefore, it's not surprising that growth and nursing are also closely related to each other. As studies of mammals and hydra have demonstrated, evolution does not tinker with some molecules. If something works well, it tends to stay around and continue to be used across eons of time.

Alternatively, some neuropeptides have been modified only slightly but often for related purposes. For example, most animal venoms are derived from neuropeptide-related precursors, and some may have originated from brain peptides that initially appeared at least 100 million years ago and have since been undergoing modification and mutation. Yet, some venoms still retain the ability to perform functions that their evolutionary parent molecule still performs, such as an insulin-like ability to control blood glucose levels. Because of this shared evolutionary history, venoms extracted from species that range from very simple single-celled organisms to very complex animals and plants have become popular tools for scientists studying how human neuropeptide neurons function. During the past 30 years, these studies have demonstrated that there are more than 100 different neuropeptide neurotransmitters in our brain and body. These neuropeptides are found at very low concentrations and are very potent.

This chapter focuses on neuropeptide neurotransmitters whose actions in the brain were discovered through the euphoric and pain-relieving effects of one of the most powerful and addicting class of drugs ever known. By way of contrast, it also discusses the pain-relieving effects of a few drugs that do not work through these neuropeptides but, rather, through a very different mechanism. The contrast is interesting in what it tells us about these neuropeptides in the context of the full arsenal of mechanisms that the body uses to protect itself from pain and other distress.

OPIATES AND OPIATE-LIKE NEUROTRANSMITTERS

The euphoric and sleep-producing effects of opiates, which are derived from the poppy plant, were well-known to ancient civilizations. Around 4000 BCE, for example, the Sumerians

(Babylonians) carved pictures of the poppy plant into tablets inscribed with the words *hul* ("joy") and *gil* ("plant"). In the classical literature of Virgil (1st century BCE), *Somnus*, the Roman god of sleep (a translation of the Greek *Hypnos*), was sometimes described as carrying poppies and an opium container from which he poured juice into the eyes of the sleeper. Chinese legend has the poppy plant springing up from the earth where the Buddha's eyelids had fallen after he cut them off to prevent sleep.

The first specific medical use of opium was described in the Ebers papyrus of ancient Egypt (about 1500 BCE), where it is presented as a remedy for excessive crying in children. The substance was important for Greek medicine as well. According to Galen, the last of the great Greek physicians (2nd century CE), opium was an antidote to poison and venoms and cured headaches, vertigo, deafness, blindness, muteness, coughs, colic, and jaundice. He also noted its recreational use at the time, commenting on the widespread sale of opium cakes and candies.

Various opium preparations, usually as extractions into some type of alcoholic beverage, were later developed, including Dr. Thomas Sydenham's version of *laudanum* during the 17th century, which contained 2 ounces of strained opium, 1 ounce of saffron, and a dram of cinnamon and cloves dissolved in a pint of Canary wine. The 19th century author Thomas De Quincey purchased laudanum for a toothache and then spent rest of his life taking the drug and writing about his experiences with it (e.g., in *Confessions of an English Opium-Eater*, 1821). Another preparation was paregoric, a combination of opium, camphor, and anise oil that was developed in the mid-20th century for the treatment of diarrhea in infants.

Meanwhile, in about 1806, when working as a pharmacist's apprentice in Paderborn, Germany, Frederich Serturner isolated the primary active ingredient in opium and named it morphium after *Morphius*, the Greek god of dreams and the son of Hypnos. Later investigations discovered an additional active ingredient called codeine, the Greek word for "poppy head." In 1874, chemists attached two acetyl groups to morphine and produced heroin, which Bayer Labs marketed in 1898 as a supposedly nonaddicting substitute for codeine. The two additional acetyl groups made heroin more potent than morphine because they increased its lipid-solubility and allowed more of the drug to enter the brain very rapidly. Heroin is, in short, just a chemical trick to get morphine into the brain faster. But once inside the brain, heroin can do nothing on its own; first it must be converted into morphine by enzymes that remove those two additional acetyl groups. Then, as the molecule originally found in the poppy seed, it can act to produce pain relief or euphoria.

The effects of morphine, codeine, and heroin in the brain are dose-related. Small doses produce drowsiness, decreased anxiety and inhibition, reduced concentration, muscle relaxation, pain relief, depressed respiration, constricted pupils, nausea, and a decreased cough reflex, which is why codeine found its way into cough suppressants. At slightly higher doses, morphine and heroin can produce a state of intense elation or euphoria.

Their euphoragenic property is related to their speed of entry into the brain, which again is directly related to their lipid-solubility. The euphoric effect is most enhanced by injecting these drugs into a vein, thus greatly accelerating their entry into the brain, and results in the "kick, bang, or rush" that addicts describe as an abdominal orgasm, a sudden flush of warmth localized in the pit of the stomach. Interestingly, the user does not experience this rush if the drug is smoked, sniffed, or swallowed because of the much slower absorption and entry into the brain via these methods of administration.

Has always, the Law of Initial Value determines how a person responds to a drug. For example, in well-adjusted, emotionally stable, pain free people, morphine may produce restlessness and anxiety. In contrast, elation most often occurs in users who are either abnormally depressed or highly excited. At very high doses of morphine, the profound depression of brain activity deepens into a state of unconsciousness that can be fatal. Respiratory depression caused by inhibition of the brain's breathing centers is the ultimate cause of death.

The effects of morphine eventually led many scientists to predict that the brain possesses its own endogenous opiate-like neurotransmitters and its own complement of endogenous opiate receptors in the brain. In the mid-1970's research confirmed that the brain and body do indeed contain some endogenous morphine-like peptides and christened them "endorphins." These peptides control our experience of pain by stopping the flow of pain signals into our brains, and this action is enhanced by the taking of opiate drugs like morphine, as well as by engaging in activities (e.g., jogging) that can produce an "endorphin high."

Morphine-like neuropeptides, as well as many other psychoactive chemicals capable of acting on the brain's neurotransmitter receptors, may also originate from many commonly consumed foods, including milk; eggs; cheese; grains such as rice, wheat, rye, and barley; spinach; mushrooms; pumpkin; meat; and various fish such as tuna, sardine, herring, and salmon. Dairy products in particular contain a protein known as casein, which enzymes in your intestines can easily convert into beta-caseomorphine. When newborns start nursing, the milk protein casein is converted to β-caseomorphine, which can easily pass out of the immature gut and into the brain (both are still lacking viable barriers at this young age) and produce euphoria. The pleasurable feeling produced by this opiate-like compound in newborn mammals after their first taste of milk is believed to encourage the infant to return again and again for nourishment. Adults do not experience this euphoria after drinking milk because of the presence of intact blood–gut and blood–brain barriers. Perhaps if we could experience the euphoria of heroin and the pain relief of morphine with each glass of milk, then dairy cows would likely only be sold on the black market!

A final note: The opiate-containing poppy seeds that many people consume as part of their morning muffin or bagel have no pain-relieving or other psychoactive effect because the dose is far too low. Nonetheless, it is possible to detect traces of morphine and codeine in the urine within a few hours after consumption.

A STUDY IN CONTRAST: OTHER DRUGS FOR PAIN RELIEF

Can other drugs control some types of pain better than opiates? In the process of answering this question, neuroscientists have learned a lot about how the brain experiences and controls the sensation of pain. Pain is categorized according to the types of neuronal fibers that carry the pain signal to your brain. For example, sharp pain is mediated by fast thick fibers; aching pain is mediated by small slow fibers. We have all experienced these two unique types of pain, yet the experience of each type is very personal. Pain is increased by our feelings and expectations, such as fatigue, anxiety, fear, boredom, and anticipation of more pain. Personality plays a role in the experience of pain as well. For example, introverts are generally found to have a lower pain threshold than extroverts. Interestingly, redheads are more sensitive to pain than blondes, who are more sensitive than brunettes. Perhaps the genetic information that allows us to process pain information may travel near the genes for hair color.

Pain involving muscles and bones is most often treated with salicylates. The name is derived from the Latin *salix*, meaning willow, which harks back to the Greek practice 2400 years ago of using extracts of the willow tree, *Filipendula ulmaria*, with coriander, *Coriandrum sativum*, for the treatment of pain, gout, and other conditions. Some 2000 years later, Native Americans were using a tea brewed from willow bark to reduce fever. The salicy-lates were rediscovered in Europe around 1763, when Englishman Reverend Edward Stone prepared an extract of willow bark for 50 patients with varying illnesses and found the results to be "uniformly excellent." In the 19th century, the active ingredient in these preparations was isolated and identified as salicylic acid.

It is interesting to compare two compounds introduced by Bayer laboratories in Germany at this time in history. We've already encountered one of them: diacetylmorphine, or heroin. The other was acetylsalicylic acid, or aspirin, which is now the most widely used analgesic. Both drugs are rapidly transformed to their original form after absorption—that is, they are con-verted to their active forms by removal of the acetyl groups. Bayer had discovered two very important pain-relieving medica-tions that would have a dramatic impact on the lives of millions of people around the world.

How does aspirin differ from morphine? Aspirin has three main beneficial effects in your body. It blocks pain in the mild-to-moderate range, and it reduces both inflammation and fever. Its effects on pain derive from its actions not on neuropeptides, such as the endogenous opiates in the brain, but on a local hor-mone called prostaglandin that is released at the site of bodily pain. When a cell in your body is damaged or injured, prota-glandins are rapidly synthesized and released from the injured cells. Prostaglandins help mediate pain in the injured areas. They sensitize your pain-sensing neurons to mechanical stimulation, causing you to stop moving and rest the injured part of your body. Aspirin relieves your pain by blocking the synthesis of prostaglandins; it essentially stops their release and prevents the transmission of pain signals. Therefore, its analgesic actions are only effective in tissues where prostaglandin formation occurs. Its effectiveness in reducing inflammation, the basis for its use in the treatment of arthritis pain, occurs for the same reason: It prevents the synthesis of prostaglandins in inflamed joints. Aspirin can do nothing, however, to alleviate pain originating from tissue in which prostaglandins are not involved in the generation of the pain signals. For example, pain that originates within the organs, such as the intestines or liver, does not rely on the formation and release of prostaglandins. Under these conditions, opiates, which act directly on the brain's endogenous morphine-like peptide receptors, provides much better pain relief.

Aspirin is not the only popular choice for the relief of minor aches and pains. Another is acetaminophen, primarily known by its trade name, Tylenol. Its pain-relief mechanism has not been fully determined, but recent evidence indicates that acetaminophen increases the brain's production of the endogenous marijuana-like neurotransmitter anandamide discussed earlier. Anandamide can, in fact, reduce the experience of pain. Patients who suffering from the pain associated with multiple sclerosis, for example, have found that a combination of marijuana and acetaminophen or aspirin provides significant relief of their symptoms. Thus, the future of pain treatment may involve a similar combination of drugs that target multiple brain neu-rotransmitter systems simultaneously.

Aspirin's ability to reduce fever results from the blockade of prostaglandin synthesis in the hypothalamus, the part of your brain that controls body temperature. The production and release of prostaglandins in the hypothalamus are activated in response to the entry of bacteria or viruses into your body. The fever you experience is induced by pieces of the bacterial cell walls and the RNA inside of the viruses. Where do all of these particles of viruses and bacteria originate? They come from you. In fact, if you were to count all of the cells on and inside of you that are not actually YOU, they would number in the tens of trillions, with approximately 1 million of these microbes living within every square centimeter of your skin! That means that for every 1 of your big human cells, roughly 100 to 1000 little bugs live alongside. The next time you look in a mirror, just imagine the multitude of individual genomes that are reflected back to you. These little bugs that have hitched their fortunes to you contribute to your good health as well as to your sickness. As our species and theirs evolved, we have all established some rules to govern our cohabitation, and most of the time every-thing works out fine; however, like an unpredictable roommate, these bugs can turn against us, and their impact on brain function can be profound. Without doubt, they share our body's exposure to the drugs and foods we consume, although no one has yet determined what role they play in how we (which would include all of their cells and all of our cells) respond to a particular drug or nutrient. All that is known is that when we experience a fever, aspirin is effective in reducing it by blocking the prostaglandins that these bugs activate in our hypothalamus.

Our ancestors were intimately aware of the beneficial effects of other plant extracts besides those from the willow tree for the treatment of pain. For example, myrrh—isolated from the dried resin in the bark of *Commiphora myrrha*, a shrub found in Somalia and throughout the Middle East—was historically used in liniments, including in Chinese medicine, to treat the symptoms of arthritis and as an antiseptic ointment. It may be slightly more potent than morphine and may act via central endogenous opiate receptors to produce analgesia. Another resin, frankincense, can be extracted from the *Boswellia sacra* tree and exhibits a mild anti-inflammatory action similar to aspirin. In ancient times, frankincense and myrrh were commonly used together as a salve to relieve *post partum* pain and to reduce bleeding after delivery. They were also burned as incense and, as immortalized in the Christmas story of the three wise men, were highly valued as a gift.

SUMMARY

As you've seen, we learn much about a particular neurotransmitter system by examining the effects of drugs that selectively enhance or inhibit its function in the brain. Mother Nature provided a wonderful tool in the form of morphine; its effects on our brains have guaranteed that mankind will never lose interest in this drug. Opiates clearly play a very important role in the experience of pain—both psychological and physiological—in our brain and body. Our endogenous opiate systems reward us with euphoria when we activate them by ingesting wonderful-tasting food, running 50 miles, or injecting heroin.

Our ancestors were, of course, ignorant of the neurobiology of opiates or prostaglandin synthesis inhibitors. In the distant past, when a person felt pain—particularly in the absence of evidence of injury—spiritual healers or medicine men developed fanciful myths to explain the cause of the pain, treated it with a decoction from the willow tree or myrrh shrub, and were often rewarded with elevated positions in their communities when their treatments seemed to magically make the pain go away and produced such an intense feeling of joy at the same time. With the advance of modern science, we know more about the mechanisms of pain and about the reasons why some drugs are better at treating it than others.

Overall, however, our knowledge about the human brain remains quite incomplete, and in the gulf of what we have yet to discover lay numerous unanswered questions and unproven theories about various aspects of our experience as emotional, sentient beings. Countless myths have been invented to fill this gulf of ignorance, and among these myths, as discussed in Chapter 9, are those concerning normal age-related mental decline and the benefits of herbal remedies purported to restore function in the aging brain.

Brain Enhancement and Other Magical Beliefs

Our brains change throughout our lives and not always for the better. Why do they change? There are many causes of cognitive decline, including drugs that stimulate GABA receptors too well, calcium channel blockers, dementia and various diseases of the brain and body, head injury, hormone imbalance, dietary nutrient deficiency or excess, heavy metal toxicity, sleep deprivation, and prolonged stress, to name only a few. The treatments are as varied as the causes. The good news is that sometimes these treatments are relatively effective at assisting the compensation or recovery of a diseased or injured brain.

In contrast, no treatments are currently available that can reverse one of the biggest causes of cognitive decline: normal aging.

Put another way, it is impossible to enhance the function of a normal brain as it ages, despite the recent research that has been focused on achieving this goal. This fact has not deterred con artists from placing numerous advertisements on the Internet that claim their products are effective brain boosters or cognition enhancers. In general, these products take advantage of the ability of stimulants to enhance performance. Notice the difference in my terms—stimulants only enhance performance, not intelligence or cognitive function. The classic brain stimulants already discussed, coffee, amphetamine, or nicotine, might improve performance, engaging certain neurotransmitters in the process, but they do not raise one's IQ score, and they do not stop normal age-related cognitive decline. The continuing myth of cognitive enhancers relies on the tendency of people to confuse faster performance with real intelligence. However ...

FASTER IS NOT SMARTER

One interesting and surprising predictor of intelligence is finger-tapping speed, which turns out to be influenced by the level of dopamine in the forebrain. Research on the brain's timing system, its internal ticking clock, has often pointed to the important role of dopamine in controlling the timing of movement and information processing speed. People who tap their fingers fast usually also think fast, and their increased processing speed correlates with their IQ score. The obvious prediction then is that these people also have a high level of dopamine in their forebrain. By contrast, people with Parkinson's disease have reduced levels of dopamine in their forebrain, move slowly, and in the advanced stages of the disease, suffer with a bothersome slowing of mental function. Their finger-tapping speed is commensurately slow as well.

So how to explain why drinking coffee or taking some other stimulant does not make us more intelligent? Your own computer can help answer this question. You are likely using a computer that processes data at gigabytes per second; a few years ago, you may have used one that processed at only megabytes per second. Your computer today is not smarter, just faster. Your brain is much like this, and dopamine seems to be responsible for the clock speed that is coupled to your processing speed. Your finger-tapping speed may correlate with your IQ, but consuming stimulants such as coffee or amphetamine-like drugs to increase dopamine release will only arouse you and speed your thinking; it will not raise your IQ even one point higher. Now imagine you were to consume heroin or alcohol, drugs that are known as depressants. These drugs slow you down and make you act and feel fuzzy-headed and stupid. However, when their effects wear off, your IQ has not lost any points.

Why not just take a lot of stimulants and increase your brain's processing speed to the point where you appear to be a genius, even if you're not? The answer is that your brain is probably already functioning almost as fast as is safe. Most of us can push the processing speed a little without risk. Unfortunately, the neural processing speed in our brains is already just a few extra action potentials per second away from a full-blown seizure.

Indeed, your brain works so fast that you are always vulnerable to seizures in response to many different stimuli, such as a small head injury, a stroke, rapidly flashing lights, a tumor, vascular abnormalities, small hemorrhages, and so forth. Given the limitations of our brain physiology and chemistry, we are probably as smart as we possibly can be at this time in our species' evolution.

The human brain is a product of its complex and multimillion-year history of solving the problems of survival for its host feeding tube in an ever-changing environment. Some of our brain structures evolved to solve one problem at one point in the evolution of our species and then ended up being used for another, usually related, problem. Overall, your brain is fairly fast, but surprisingly, it's not too efficient, which is probably why stimulants can make us perform some tasks a little better. We compensate for inefficiency by slightly increasing our sensory and information processing speed. For all of these reasons, and so many more, the brain shows no evidence of being designed in any intelligent manner; it simply works as best as it needs to work to allow us to survive and thrive in our current environment. If our current environment changes too much or too quickly, then there is no guarantee that our species will survive. After all, over 95% of all species that are known to have existed on this planet have already become extinct. No species has had a lock on having a perfect body or brain that allowed it to survive in all environments. The Nobel Prize-winning French biologist François Jacob wrote that "evolution is a tinkerer" that did not intentionally create anything beyond what was needed at the time for survival. This is why we, and every other species on the planet, are always vulnerable to significant changes in our environment.

In the meantime, we are pretty much stuck with what our brains are capable of achieving in the here and now, and that capability does change with age regardless of the substances we might take to speed our mental performance. Thus far, no one has been able to design a drug therapy that can make a person smarter in any real and long-lasting way, other than temporarily increasing processing speed. So if we look at the so-called memory boosters and cognitive enhancers on the market today, we see that they usually contain caffeine, sugar, and a few extra vitamins that together do very little except pep you up and make you a little poorer. At this point in time in the 21st century, nothing— let me repeat that with emphasis, *nothing*—exists that can truly make you more intelligent and that can stop your brain from aging, so save your money. Indeed, the most recent evidence is that taking high supplemental doses of vitamins might actually undermine the benefits of a good diet on your brain function.

MOM KNOWS BEST

But do not despair—we can probably age better and more slowly and retain our existing level of cognitive function longer if we feed our brains properly. Clearly, one's diet and activity level can have a positive or negative effect on brain function. A diet high in saturated fat decreases your brain's capacity for learning, decreases the level of the important growth factor brain-derived neurotrophic factor (BDNF) (which is vital to learning), and worsens your ability to recover from traumatic brain injury. In contrast, a modest amount of exercise can increase the level of BDNF and attenuate the effects of a high-fat diet on the brain and can even increase the expression of genes that underlie brain plasticity and recovery from injury. Thus, the solution to aging well is exactly what you've heard from your mom, probably because she's not that interested in making a profit on you: eat healthy and exercise, both in moderation.

I'd add one more piece of advice that your mother likely would not think to mention: eat just enough sugar to support your brain's needs. Somewhere in our evolutionary history, we lost the ability to make sugar from fat; unlike a few lucky animals, humans cannot perform this metabolic trick. Just think what a wonderful world it would be if you could convert your body fat into sugar for your brain; you would never feel hungry while your body busily burned up all of your fat. But you're not able to accomplish this feat. Instead, you must obtain most of the sugar you need from your diet, and your brain uses it to make energy for one important process: so that your neurons can maintain their resting "membrane potential." Without this electrical potential, which exists across a cell membrane, the activity of your brain would stop and you would quickly die. Thus, in the morning when you awaken from a long sleep and a long period of fasting, your brain wants you to eat a donut or a bagel. There is a reason that these foods are so popular, and you can lay the blame mostly on norepinephrine's actions within the feeding center of your hypothalamus. This mechanism works nicely: first thing in the morning, you eat lots of simple, easily digestible sugars, and your brain rewards you with a good feeling by increasing the release of dopamine and a surge of endogenous opiates. Your brain also uses sugar to produce two neurotransmitters that are critical for learning and memory, glutamate and acetylcholine. Sugar thus facilitates arousal and memory storage, two things you need from your brain throughout the day.

Impaired glucose regulation correlates with impaired learning in aged humans and in people with Alzheimer's disease, particularly during its earliest stages. Scientists have recently discovered that the inability of specific brain regions to use glucose appropriately and efficiently in fact precedes the degeneration of those same brain regions decades later. Would eating more sugar prevent dementia? Unfortunately, no. Nor will eating more sugar than the brain needs make oneself smarter. Consuming large amounts of sugar is also not healthy for your pancreas or cardiovascular system; thus, what's good for the brain is not always good for the other organs of your body. Therefore, you should eat enough sugar to keep your brain in good working order but not so much that the rest of your body rebels. Now if you could just work on that incessant breathing problem of yours, you and your sugar-enriched brain could be good to go for a very long time.

THE PERILS OF OXYGEN

Your mother's advice about eating healthy has a deeper story behind it. The food we eat must be metabolized, a process that requires the oxygen in the air we breathe. Unfortunately, our most basic acts of survival, breathing and eating, are what age our bodies and our brains. If this sounds like the proverbial damned-if-you-do, damned-if-you-don't scenario, well, it sort of is, and yet somehow our species has managed to survive this challenge for several hundred millennia.

Like most other animals on this planet, we humans acquire energy for our biochemical machinery by breaking down the carbon bonds found in fats, sugars, and proteins and then gobbling as much energy from the process as possible. The fact that we do this so inefficiently means that much of the energy in our food is lost as heat. This process also leaves our cells with left-over carbon atoms. The problem is what to with all of this carbon waste. More than 2 billion years ago, the solution for a small independently living single-celled organism, which might have closely resembled our own mitochondria (the furnace that handles almost all of our cells' energy production needs), was to combine these left-over carbons with a readily available gas, oxygen, and to expel the product as a gas called carbon dioxide. Thus, thanks to our current symbiotic relationship with the descendents of these ancient bacteria, our mitochondria, the way our bodies obtain energy to live is as follows: carbon bonds come into the front end of our feeding tubes in the form of fats, carbohydrates, and proteins; we then extract energy and excrete the residue as carbon dioxide and water vapor.

This process succeeded because oxygen was so abundant in the distant past; in addition, because this process was so much more efficient than any other energy-generating mechanisms available at the time, it likely assisted the evolution of single-celled organisms to multicellular plants and animals. But because oxygen is also exceedingly toxic to cells, it must be utilized very carefully and conservatively. Indeed, scientists have recently discovered that the genes that control energy metabolism have been highly conserved across millions of years of evolution, from yeast to humans, and that these genes influence the rate of the aging process. It was also discovered many years ago that the better able a species was at defending itself from the oxygen required for energy metabolism, the longer that species tended to live. Essentially, the better we negotiate our energy–oxygen exchange with our indwelling mitochondria, the longer and healthier we live as a single individual and as a species. Disrupt the balance in this exchange, and the impact can be deleterious. For example, studies suggest that disruption of the balance of forces between our mitochondria and the nuclei of our neurons may underlie a wide variety of illnesses, including Alzheimer's disease, Parkinson's disease, bipolar disorder, amyotrophic lateral sclerosis, multiple sclerosis, and depression.

In general, the hemoglobin in our blood does a decent job of regulating the oxygen levels near the individuals cells of our bodies so that those cells have the oxygen they need for respiration but not too much to kill them outright. These cells have also evolved numerous anti-oxidant systems that would allow us live to be 115 years old, if we were lucky and ate very, very little food. But most of us are not that lucky, and most of us eat all of the time and just keep on breathing, making ourselves vulnerable to the consequences of oxygen. Thus our bodies and our brains age more rapidly.

With normal aging, because we insist on eating and breathing, tissue-damaging molecules called oxygen-free radicals are formed by our mitochondria. Free radicals are not always harmful; however, they become more prevalent with age and may slowly overwhelm our natural anti-oxidant systems, destroying our neurons and just about every other cell in our bodies. According to another recent discovery, the overproduction of these oxygen-free radicals may encourage cancer cells to metastasize and move around the body. Think about the unbelievable irony of this process: The mitochondrial power plant that resides in quite large numbers in every cell of our bodies is actively injuring those cells by the very process of trying to keep them alive. It turns out that each species' maximum lifespan may be determined by how many free radicals are produced by the hundreds of mitochondria that live in each of their cells. We are, indeed, always our own worst enemy.

My recommendation with regard to healthy aging is to eat less food, thus reducing the likelihood of making oxygen-free radicals, and to enhance the anti-oxidant processes you inherited by eating foods rich in anti-oxidants, particularly colorful fruits and lots of vegetables. Doing so will protect your cells and slow the aging process, and you will live longer. In addition, according to other recent studies, limiting the amount of protein we consume will reduce our chances of getting cancer. Eating less will not, however, prolong our lives beyond the normal maximal lifespan expected for humans. Nor do the benefits of a low-calorie diet necessarily extend to our brains as we age. For example, most of us will still suffer with age-related memory problems. Furthermore, diet restriction may actually accelerate the brain's degeneration and death in people with amyotrophic lateral sclerosis or Lou Gehrig's disease.

ELIXIRS FOR THE AGING BRAIN?

Interestingly, some substances that we would not typically consider to be healthy can have beneficial effects on *how* the brain ages. For example, nicotine may be neuroprotective, as may the contents of tobacco smoke, which contains very high levels of chemicals that are efficient chelators of heavy metals. There is, in any case, a reduced incidence of Parkinson's disease in people who smoke. Consumption of large volumes of caffeine-containing drinks is also associated with reduced incidence of Parkinson's disease. The regular consumption of alcohol, primarily beer, has been correlated with a later onset of Alzheimer's disease; this might result from the ability of alcohol to reduce blood levels of cholesterol, which is directly correlated with a greater risk of dementia in later life. As noted in Chapter 5, research conducted by Dr. Yannick Marchalant in my laboratory has shown that marijuana can be quite beneficial in reducing the onset of age-related diseases that involve brain inflammation, including multiple sclerosis, Parkinson's disease, Alzheimer's disease, Huntington's disease, and a variety of autoimmune diseases. A few recent studies have suggested that people who smoked marijuana in the 1960s are today somewhat less likely to develop Alzheimer's disease.

This is not an advertisement for you to take up smoking cigarettes and pot or drinking beer and coffee because you think doing so will save you from the ravages of these diseases. I mention the beneficial effects of these substances only to emphasize a point: Scientists know about the correlations between the regular use of these popular herbal-based drugs and the reduced incidence of some age-related brain disorders because millions of people have administered billions of doses of these substances during the past thousand years, but only relatively recently has careful record-keeping allowed us to observe the quite subtle, yet very consistent, benefits provided by these drugs. Thus, it is only because these drugs are so widely abused that we've noticed their positive effects on the brain. There may be wonderful new drugs to be discovered in, say, cauliflower or haggis, but too few people have been willing to eat them in sufficient numbers and for a sufficient period of time for epidemiologists to take notice of their hidden benefits on our brain, if they exist.

Many plants do contain compounds that should be able to enhance your brain's performance. For example, potatoes, tomatoes, and eggplants contain solanine and α-chaconine that can enhance the action of acetylcholine. Yet eating these foods does not improve your memory. Your mood should be enhanced slightly by eating fava beans (with or without a fine Chianti) because they contain L-DOPA, a precursor to the production of dopamine, the reward chemical in your brain. The reason that eating fava beans does not make you feel happier is because it is highly unlikely that these ingredients are able to get to their site of potential action at a sufficient concentration that would produce a noticeable effect on brain function. This might explain why no one is hawking potatoes and eggplants as a cure for dementia.

However, I can assure you that someone somewhere is now selling "*THE CURE*" for mental decline. I truly wish that a cure did exist; I'd be first in line to get it. We would all prefer to defy the aging process by simply taking a pill and to be able to eat with impunity everything we desire rather than to follow our mothers' prosaic advice about moderate, healthy eating. But again, and alas, no such cure exists. The fact that science has not yet invented a true brain enhancer has not stopped people from selling drugs, ancient elixirs, unusual therapies with mystical names, and hundreds of books that all boast of the properties of this or that miracle, age-defying brain booster. If someone might gain financially from your gullibility, then what he or she is selling is probably useless, and there is no guarantee that it is safe. However, if you really need something to maintain your delusion that an anti-aging cure for your brain exists, just read on.

GINKGO BILOBA AND OTHER HERBAL "REMEDIES"

The Internet is bursting with claims that pills and drinks containing extracts of the Ginkgo biloba plant may neutralize free radicals, dilate the blood vessels in your brain, make you smarter, and slow the aging process. How? The claim is that Gingko biloba increases the function of acetylcholine neurons and thereby enhances memory and arouses and improves attentional ability.

Dozens of clinical trials have examined the cognitive effects of gingko plant extracts in humans. A great majority of the studies indicating a positive effect have involved patients who have a mild-to-moderate memory impairment, frequently with a diagnosis of early Alzheimer's disease. Most experiments tested learning and memory, less often attention. Most of the subjects were selected and tested long after they began using gingko products, typically several months; thus, their cognitive level before using gingko is unknown. This fact may have introduced a bias. For example, higher scores on the memory and learning tests may have come from subjects with better cognitive abilities who could read and understand articles suggesting that gingko might help them or who were better able to remember to take the drug. These critical factors were never considered by the authors of these studies. Testing any drug that claims to enhance cognitive function will have this kind of potential bias in the choice of subjects. At the very least, researchers need to give cognitive function tests both before and after the patients start taking gingko, or else the experimental results showing improved cognitive function from the use of this substance are suspect.

There is another serious problem with clinical trials on plant extracts: determining how much of a given extract a patient should be given, and which extract is the effective one. When ancient Chinese herbalists recommended that their patients take ginkgo biloba, or any number of other plant extracts that have been prescribed during that past 2 millennia, they always estimated dosage based on past experience. But plants are complicated organisms that make a large variety of molecules, some of which are active in the brain, some of which are not active in the brain but are quite nutritious, and some of which are just inert. Moreover, the contents of plants change according to growing conditions. How much of any particular extract should therefore be taken by a person who seeks the benefit that ginkgo might offer? No one knows! The studies necessary to establish a truly effective dose have never been performed rigorously.

The little research that exists suggests that the ingredients of these herbals have numerous potential mechanisms of action on a variety of neural systems. Unfortunately, there is a lack of unanimity in the research because of various methodological problems in many of these studies, such as inadequate sample size (the number of subjects in the study) and a lack of a double-blind, placebo-controlled paradigm, the gold standard of modern scientific research. This paradigm means that no one involved in a drug trial—including its investigators and its subjects—knows which tested substance, whether an active drug or a placebo (usually an inactive form of the drug under study or a sugar pill), is being administered. The purpose of this approach has to do, again, with bias: to keep investigator and subject bias from influencing the trial's results.

In fact, on the rare occasion that this standard has been applied to studies on alternative medicines such as gingko biloba, the results have not been positive. For example, a pair of very large clinical trials that followed the health of more than 3000 people of various ages for 8 years clearly demonstrated that gingko biloba cannot influence the development of age-related memory problems. Another trial indicated that the use of gingko may actually be harmful by increasing an individual's risk of nonhemorrhagic stroke, which is when a blood vessel in the brain becomes blocked and shuts off blood flow.

These are, however, just a handful of studies, and much more high-quality research needs to occur before the effectiveness of gingko biloba and other herbal products is irrefutably proven or disproven. In the meantime, most manufacturers of these products prefer to err on the side of selling diluted samples to avoid any toxic side effects and potential law suits from people who survive the experience. But that's still no guarantee that the samples are safe. Unacceptably high levels of pesticides and carcinogens have, for example, been found in a large percentage of imported samples.

These concerns aside, many people are convinced that they benefit from substances like gingko biloba or the countless other products on the market that promise enhanced cognitive function. Why? Because, in brief, they want these drugs to do something, anything, so they fool themselves into thinking that they do. We all are subject to this thinking from time to time, and it is identified by three little words.

THE PLACEBO EFFECT

When it comes to alternative medicines and therapies that, like gingko biloba, claim to enhance your brain function, never underestimate the power of your own expectations. Not only does your brain influence how you think and feel, but the nature of your thoughts and expectations can influence how your brain and body functions. Thus, if you expect that a drug will act in a certain way on your brain and behavior, then it is much more likely to do so, at least for a while; this is the essence of the placebo effect. It's ironic, and possibly way too convenient, that your brain decides for itself how it will experience the drug that it has decided to take.

Much has been written about the value of the placebo effect in the practice of medicine, but how this effect emerges and whether it can be controlled are issues that not yet understood. Essentially, scientists have analyzed the effect based on results of placebo-controlled studies of actual drugs on the brain or have compared only the effects of a placebo against the consequences of no treatment at all. Their findings have been intriguing, if still largely inconclusive. However, in one area of study that is not directly related to an actual treatment, the findings are more definitive. Numerous meta-analyses (which are later analyses of other researchers' data) have shown that only the perception of pain can be statistically demonstrated to be influenced by our minds, which scientists refer to as the emergent property of our brains. This influence of our thoughts and expectations on how we experience pain is a true placebo effect.

In one study, published in late 2008, scientists measured pain perception in two groups of people, devout practicing Catholics and professed atheists and agnostics, while they viewed an image of the Virgin Mary or the painting of *Lady with an Ermine* by Leonardo da Vinci. The devout Catholics perceived electrical pulses to their hand as being less painful when they looked at the Virgin Mary than when they looked at the da Vinci work. In contrast, the atheists and agnostics derived no pain relief while viewing either picture. MRI scans demonstrated that the Catholics' pain relief was associated with greatly increased brain activity in their right ventrolateral prefrontal cortex. This brain region is believed to be involved in controlling our emotional response to sensory stimuli, such as pain. Perhaps this study has, in fact, shown us the location of the placebo effect.

Other studies using brain imaging techniques to show correlations between brain activity and the extent of reported placebo effects have demonstrated that some people show greater placebo responses than others, but that everyone appears to be capable of having such a response. There is also increasing proof that the use of placebos might benefit people with Parkinson's disease, depression, and anxiety. In the future, with better testing measures, scientists will likely demonstrate how the placebo effect influences many aspects of our health. In short, the placebo effect is real; we simply do not understand entirely how it works, but the evidence thus far is truly remarkable, particularly with regard to pain. Some people are able to block incoming pain signals or alter how they are perceived. And without a doubt, your mind can make the experience of pain more or less agonizing depending on how you feel—for example, are you fatigued, anxious, fearful, or bored; do you expect more painful experiences to be coming soon?

As noted, your mind also plays a major role in how drugs affect you. Although we don't yet know how the placebo effect works in the brain to influence this process, we do know that it does come into play and sometimes in surprising ways. For example, the color of the pill you take influences your expectation of what it will do to you. Obviously, pills can be made any color, yet most people like their anti-anxiety pills to be blue or pink or some other soft, warm color; they prefer their powerful anti-cancer pills to be red or brightly colored. Americans do not like black or brown pills, in contrast to the preference of people in the United Kingdom, or Europe. Thus, almost everything that Americans buy over the counter is a small white, round pill. Yet big pills, or pills with odd shapes, are also assumed to be more powerful, or just simply better, than tiny round pills. Sometimes, a simple change in color or shape restores a drug's ability to produce a placebo effect. And sometimes, the effect comes from the pill-taking regimen. For example, you expect that when you are instructed to take a medication only during a full moon, or only every other Thursday, it must be extremely, almost mystically, effective. Herbalists often take advantage of this concept by recommending odd or excessive dosages of peculiar-looking pills or foul-smelling potions. We all want to believe that the pills we take will help us feel and function better; fortunately, thanks to the poorly understood phenomenon of the placebo effect, we do sometimes, but only for a while, benefit even from the most bogus of potions and pills. As Tinker Bell said, "You just have to believe!" If all you're getting is a sugar pill, then does it really matter whether you're fooled into believing the lie? Possibly; it depends on the cost of the sugar pills and the risk one assumes by not taking a medicine of proven effectiveness in a timely fashion for a medical condition. The risk of taking substances that merely promise the elusive Holy Grail of enhanced, age-defying brain function may be no less dire, depending on the true nature of the "sugar" that's in them.

SUMMARY

It's so easy to be fooled. Our brains are not as perfect as we would like them to be, and so we keep looking for the magic pill or potion that will make us smarter and prevent the inexorable effects of aging. As long as we keep searching, someone will be there to sell it to us, and we'll stand in line to buy it, none the wiser or healthier and a lot poorer. Still, that does not mean that there is no hope. You have seen that there is one very simple and money-saving thing that we can do to enhance our brain's performance and to slow the aging process: eat a lot less food, because you should never underestimate the power of food on your mind.

A Little Quiz

At the beginning of this book, I stated that my purpose was to demonstrate that we can use our current knowledge of how drugs and nutrients affect the brain to gain a better appreciation of how the brain works. Thus, can you answer the following questions? Which neurotransmitter system is being antagonized when you feel a complete inability to pay attention or to learn something new? Which neurotransmitter system is most likely affected by a drug that robs you of the ability to feel pleasure? Which is affected when you feel aroused? Did you answer: acetylcholine, dopamine, and norepinephrine? What do the effects of hallucinogenic drugs tell us about the serotonin system? Why does marijuana produce the "munchies?" Why does drinking alcohol slow down your brain function? How do energy drinks or chocolate bars pep you up in the afternoon? Why is morphine such an effective painkiller? What is so unhealthy about consuming lots and lots of calories?

Although your answers might not always be unerringly correct, you can see that there is a degree of predictability about how your brain responds to drugs and the food you eat. It's really not all that mysterious. As you learn more about the brain, whether from the suggested readings I've listed or from other sources, you will become a wiser consumer of both the nutrients and drugs that affect how you think and feel.

SUGGESTED READINGS

Allman, John Morgan. *Evolving Brains*. Scientific American Library, 1999.

Bausell, R. Barker. *Snake Oil Science: The truth about complementary and alternative medicine*. New York: Oxford University Press, 2007.

Courtright, David T. *Forces of Habit: Drugs and the making of the modern world*. Cambridge: Harvard University Press, 2001.

Gold, Paul E., Larry Cahill, & Gary L. Wenk. The Lowdown on Ginkgo. *Scientific American*, April, 2003.

Lane, Nick. *Oxygen: The Molecule that Made the World*. Oxford University Press, 2004.

Linden, David. *The Accidental Mind: How brain evolution has given us love, memory, dreams, and God*. Cambridge: Harvard University Press, 2007.

Meyer, Jerrold S., & Linda F. Quenzer. *Psychopharmacology: Drugs, Brain and Behavior*. Sinauer, 2005.

Miller, L.G., & W.J. Murray (Eds.). *Herbal Medicinals: A Clinicians Guide.* New York: Pharmaceutical Products Press, 1998.

Perry, Elaine, Heather Ashton, & Allan Young (Eds.). *Neurochemistry of Consciousness.* John Benjamins Publ., 2002.

Spinella, Marcello. *The Psychopharmacology of Herbal Medicines.* Cambridge: MIT Press, 2001.

INDEX

Note: Page numbers followed by "*f*" refer to figures.